HISTORIC PHOTOS OF
CORPUS CHRISTI

TEXT AND CAPTIONS BY
CECILIA GUTIERREZ VENABLE

TURNER
PUBLISHING COMPANY

This view from North Broadway Street on the bluff, looking toward the bay, features Market Hall. This building served as a place for vendors. Graduation exercises, parties, and other recreational activities were held on its second floor. The narrow building on the left was used as City Hall. Across the street is the Watts and Dunne school supplies shop.

HISTORIC PHOTOS OF
CORPUS CHRISTI

Turner Publishing Company
www.turnerpublishing.com

Copyright © 2008 Turner Publishing Company

Historic Photos of Corpus Christi

Library of Congress Control Number: 2007941389

ISBN-13: 978-1-59652-428-6

Printed in the United States of America

ISBN 978-1-68442-004-9 (hc)

CONTENTS

ACKNOWLEDGMENTS...VII

PREFACE VIII

SEAPORT TOWN THROUGH THE GILDED AGE
(1840–1893) 1

PROGRESSIVE ERA
(1894–1925) 19

THE MAKING OF A MODERN CITY
(1926–1939) 89

WAR YEARS AND AFTERMATH
(1940–1949)...117

THE GROWING METROPOLIS
(1950–1969) 155

NOTES ON THE PHOTOGRAPHS 201

Employees of the Harrison Coffee Company stand behind the counter of the coffee shop around 1910. This store opened by 1904 and was known as the Harrison's Coffee and Tea Store, which advertised the "Lowest prices on Coffees, Teas, and Fancy Groceries."

Acknowledgments

This book resulted from the cooperation and aid from many institutions and individuals. The vision, dedication, and hard work the Corpus Christi Public Libraries has invested in its collection made possible a large majority of the photographs for this publication. The library director, Herb Canales, along with Laura Garcia, Gerlinda Riojas, and Norma Gonzalez were invaluable resources. Thanks also to Rebecca Jones for her work on the photographs.

Texas A&M University-Corpus Christi Special Collections and Archives donated several images for this publication, and a special thanks to Grace Charles, who was indispensable in finding images. The input of Dr. Thomas Kreneck, Jan Weaver, and Mike Rowell were much appreciated.

The Library of Congress also provided images from its extensive holdings.

The expertise of local historians Bill and Marjorie Walraven, Anita Eisenhower, and Murphy Givens was also important in the completion of this work.

Finally, I would like to thank Audrey Flores for her dedication in getting this book together. Her hard work and perseverance were greatly appreciated. The patience and understanding of my husband, James C. (Jake) Venable, and daughter, Breanna Venable, were immeasurable.

PREFACE

At a little over a century old, Corpus Christi is a relatively young city. However, the land it rests on is thousands of years old. Through glacial formation and thaws which affected sea level change, as well as sedimentation and deposition from rivers, the land and bay emerged to form an ideal area for a port town. One of the first Native tribes to explore the Gulf Coast was the Karankawa Indians. Although nomadic, they did follow game and searched for mollusks, fish, and berries in the area. Several European expeditions landed on these shores as early as the late sixteenth century but established few permanent settlements. It would take the foresight of an ambitious entrepreneur to plant the seed for the city's development.

Henry L. Kinney arrived near Corpus Christi in 1839, fleeing from scandalous affairs and failed business dealings. This charismatic fortune hunter sought to profit from outfitting troops and found this area to be conducive to such efforts. Always a profiteer, Kinney tended to favor whoever provided the best deal. When Zachary Taylor's troops camped in the area in 1845, many people passed through town, but few stayed. In order to entice settlers to this area, Kinney held one of the first state fairs, but this scheme also failed to attract new residents. However, by 1854 Corpus Christi did have schools, churches, a strong organization for women, and fraternal lodges. When the yellow fever struck later that year, many citizens perished, but Kinney remained optimistic about the city's growth and continued to advertise the area's attributes to the Northern states and European countries. When the Civil War began, Kinney fled to Mexico in search of another pot of gold. However, he did not count on the two bullets that pierced his body when he attempted to have a rendezvous with an attached woman. He died that night in 1862.

The Civil War continued to disrupt this area. In 1863, Union forces blockaded the bay and pummeled the city with shot and shell on several occasions. At the end of the war, the town experienced a surge in population, mainly because of the cattle and sheep business. These goods could be processed and shipped to other parts of the country. When the railroad arrived around 1875, shipping, industry, and numerous businesses flocked here, along with several boosters—in particular, Elihu H. Ropes. He wanted to deepen the port, and he marketed the area as the "Chicago of the Southwest," but his dreams fell through with the Panic of 1893. He passed away during a trip to solicit Northern investors.

Despite Ropes' failure, the city grew and attracted additional railroads that promoted the area in hopes of increasing the number of people who used their rails. As more tourists and new residents entered the area, additional hotels, houses, and businesses were needed to accommodate the growing city. However, many of these new structures and entities would be destroyed in 1919 by one of the most devastating hurricanes ever to hit the area. Hundreds of people died in the disaster, and many of the buildings were washed away. The city would not recover from this economic loss for at least seven years.

The Corpus Christi port, which opened on the seventh anniversary of the hurricane—September 14, 1926—spurred growth dramatically and transformed the town into a modern city. In less than ten years after the opening of the port the population doubled, new office buildings dotted the city's landscape, and larger hotels made their home here. By the 1930s, the oil industry was an important part of the economy and cushioned the devastating effects of the Great Depression. The city's population again doubled and continued on an upward trend with the arrival of the Naval Air Station in 1941. After World War II, the oil and gas industry again boosted the economy with further development of refineries. The port also increased its capabilities and handled various exports including cotton, grains, petroleum products, crude petroleum, and natural gas. Tourism also continued to be a boon for the area and brought in many businesses.

This book captures this city's development through a montage of photographs depicting the history of the area, its people and events. No changes have been made except for touching up imperfections caused by the damage of time and cropping where necessary. The focus and clarity of many images is limited to the technology of the day and the skill of the photographer who captured them.

This project represents the sifting of thousands of photographs. Many hours of research were expended in an attempt to achieve a well-balanced view of the city's life. The only limit to this endeavor was the lack of existing images from certain segments of history. In this book, the reader is encouraged to view Corpus Christi through the lens of the past and, in doing so, perhaps gain a deeper understanding of what the city is today and where it is going.

The pipe hauled to the King Ranch for artesian wells filled most of this commercial intersection of Chaparral and Peoples streets on this 1890s day. Several businesses are also pictured, including the W. S. Rankin Grocery Store; C. C. National Bank; E. H. Caldwell's Hardware Store; Randolph Robertson's Well Machinery shop; Western Union office; and a two-story building which held a store at the street level and a hall for dancing or skating on the second floor.

Seaport Town Through the Gilded Age

(1840–1893)

A visitor reported in the 1840s that Corpus Christi consisted of only five stores and a "grog shop." The Mexican-American War proved a boon to local businesses. Zachary Taylor and his troops arrived in 1845, the year before the war began, and departed in 1846, but progress continued. The *Corpus Christi Gazette* soon began publication. Although short-lived, it provided the groundwork for subsequent newspapers. Corpus Christi received its first post office, and the following year the town was placed in Nueces County as the county seat. By 1852, the city incorporated with B. F. Neal as mayor. Soon, a jail and courthouse joined a growing number of homes and businesses.

The Civil War temporarily curtailed growth as Federal ships blockaded trade and briefly bombarded the city in 1862. Commerce resumed soon after the war, but a yellow fever epidemic in 1867 decimated about a third of Corpus Christi's citizens. Four years later, the city acquired a fire department and the Sisters of the Incarnate Word opened their doors to aid children. In 1874, this port city watched as a steamship docked near town, traveling down the newly dredged channel. A little over ten years would pass before additional tracks were laid for the San Antonio Aransas Pass Railroad.

Like Kinney in the early decades of the nineteenth century, the railroad attempted to market this area, encouraging commerce and tourists. However, the master of boosterism was Elihu Harrison Ropes, who arrived in Corpus Christi in 1888. He dredged channels, developed subdivisions, built a fabulous hotel, and marketed the area to Northern investors. Corpus Christi's population quickly expanded, which helped the Gilded Age to last a bit longer here than elsewhere. The Panic of 1893 curtailed Ropes' efforts, and Corpus Christi was left with an opulent hotel that never really opened. Despite Ropes' failure, the boom he sparked set the stage for new developments that would encourage this city's rapid growth.

The Headen and Sons building located on the corner of Schatzel and Chaparral streets around 1840 was a general merchandise store. The Headens purchased hides and sold a wide variety of goods. On October 25, 1873, the city purchased three bedsteads, a wash stand, six blankets, and a trunk for $65.50.

This is a view of David Hirsh's home. Hirsh was the founder of the successful Corpus Christi National Bank and in the 1870s became a member of the city's Board of Trade.

This 1880s early waterfront view of Laguna Street captures a few prominent family homes, including the Meuly and Robertson homes. Randolph Robertson operated a well machinery shop near Chaparral and Peoples streets. Herman Meuly operated a newsdealer, bookseller, and stationer business. Several businesses can also be seen, including the ice and power industry plant with its tall smoke stacks.

This 1882 hack driven by "Scudder" was probably owned by a prominent family, considering its fine horse and carriage. Hacks were also used by the city for various services. James M. Hunter, who owned a livery and stable on Water Street near Lawrence also owned a hack, which the city used occasionally to haul prisoners to the jail for a fee of $3.00.

The wool merchants' establishment of Arthur H. Edey & Kirsten probably operated around 1879 when Corpus Christi exported millions of pounds of wool. This lucrative business employed many workers. Shearers received two to three cents per sheep. Shepherds received $10.00 per month, plus a bushel of corn and three pounds of coffee, as well as sugar and meat. This business slowly dissipated by 1884 because of drought conditions and grassland destruction.

The DeRyee Drug store on Chaparral Street sold "Drugs, Medicines, Chemicals, Fancy and Toilet Articles, Paints, Oils and Varnishes." William DeRyee, a chemist and geologist, arrived in Corpus Christi with a Colonel Moore who was also a geologist and had a dredging boat. DeRyee made candles, soap, and other items for Moore's boat crew. Later he operated this drugstore until he retired to Mexico.

This view of Chaparral Street highlights John Woessner & Son. Next to it is the George French merchandise store, which opened in the late 1860s. French was also an active member of the city. He held positions of county treasurer, alderman, and fireman.

A horse and buggy stand in front of Dr. Alfred G. Heaney's home. A physician in Corpus Christi since 1884, he practiced medicine for 70 years before his death. Heaney was also president of Corpus Christi's fist telephone system.

A horse and cart are pictured on a Corpus Christi street. This photograph was taken by Louis de Planque, who arrived in Mexico in the late nineteenth century and opened a studio there. In 1869, he traveled to Indianola and opened another business. The following year, he opened a gallery in Corpus Christi and took several photographs of the area.

This Louis de Planque image of the Corpus Christi Volunteer Fire Department probably dates to the late 1870s. William Rogers organized the Pioneer Fire Company No. 1 in 1871 with ten men who purchased their own uniforms. Some early members were: Felix Noessel, foreman; Peter Benson, assistant foreman; L. D. Brewster, second assistant; and Ed Buckley, treasurer. This group also determined what the fire department needed and solicited funds for equipment.

This picture of Market Hall preserves the memory of February 14, 1895, "when the ground was covered with snow and sleighs were used." That Valentine's Day, three inches of snow fell in Corpus Christi. Two years later, 4.3 inches blanketed the city, the heaviest snowfall until 2004 when 4.4 inches fell. The 1897 accumulation prompted rides down the bluff with make-shift sleds and sleighs. Children also flocked to the streets to pitch snowballs at pedestrians.

The Corpus Christi Fire Department and Security Hose Co. No. 3, which covered the bluff area, stands in front of Market Hall for the start of a parade. Firemen used the second floor of Market Hall for recreation, and a fire bell dedicated on May 6, 1873, hung in the tower. The bell summoned firemen when there was a fire and also alerted citizens to the time of day, called children to school, and announced social events.

The Saint Patrick's Church, built to handle an expanding congregation, was dedicated in 1882. The church became Saint Patrick's Cathedral after a restructuring of the diocese. Unfortunately, it succumbed to a fire that swept through the building in 1938 and destroyed much of the structure. The church would later be rebuilt and the name changed to the Corpus Christi Cathedral, at the suggestion of Pope Pius XII.

The fine Alta Vista Hotel was built by Colonel Elihu Harrison Ropes to promote the city and entice investors. Unfortunately, he never opened this hotel because of the Panic of 1893, which forced him to leave town and abandon his unfinished dream. In 1905, J. J. Copley purchased the three-story hotel, which boasted 106 rooms, a bar, a dance and billiard hall, and a dining room. Never very prosperous, the hotel burned down in 1927.

This is an early view of the Corpus Christi Public School (later Old Central High School), located in the 600 block of Carancahua. Construction began in 1892 and was completed the following year. The school opened in May of 1893 and closed the same month, due to the city's financial difficulties, coupled with unexpected building costs. The school later reopened in September, but students were charged a fee to attend.

The United States Weather Bureau sits atop the George French building on the corner of Star and Chaparral streets. The weather bureau occupied two rooms on the second floor of this building. The station was forced to find another location because their original building in Indianola was destroyed by a hurricane. This station opened on February 1, 1887, and remained at this location until July 9, 1901.

PROGRESSIVE ERA

(1894–1925)

By 1894 Corpus Christi was on its way to becoming a commercial center. It already had electric and telephone service and a water system. While these amenities appeared to make the city a modern place to live and work, there were problems underlying life in this area. Public education was not adequately funded, food quality was poor, and diseases from mosquitoes flourished. The city had focused on improving business and commerce and neglected many of these ills. The Progressive Era in Corpus Christi saw the organization of several groups that brought these failings to the attention of civic leaders to force change.

The road to progress began with Dr. Arthur E. Spohn establishing a hospital on North Beach in 1895. Two years later, the Woman's Monday Club formed and diligently sought to correct the ills of the city, and it planted the seed for the La Retama club, which established a public library in 1909. A year later, trolley car service began. In 1911, the first plane to land on the beach surprised many residents. Newly installed street lights lit the city, and the next year gas from the White Point field lit the countryside. A hurricane in 1916 destroyed some of these improvements, but the city soon bounced back. Another hurricane three years later would not be so easy to overcome. The 1919 storm washed away many developments and decimated the population. The economic stability for this area was lost. The remaining six years of this period found the city cleaning and rebuilding. The disaster forced many to realize that in order to recover from this economic loss, the city needed funds to deepen the port.

A horse and wagon stand in front of Market Hall. This two-story complex built by William L. Rogers and Richard Jordan in 1871 was located on Peoples, Schatzel, and Mesquite streets and became the center of social life and business in Corpus Christi. The bottom floor housed individual retailers, while the top floor held city offices, a dance hall, and the firemen's recreation area. The building was destroyed in 1911.

This early view of Chaparral Street at Schatzel features the Corpus Christi National Bank, which moved to this location in 1891 and operated there for 69 years. Next door is the Corpus Christi Book and Stationery Company. Across the street is the Joe Mireur Shop "Outfitter to the Horse." This store sold and repaired leather goods. The city purchased various items from this store, including bridles, rope, and cremoline.

A boy with a mule-drawn water cart in the 1890s sits across the street from the Incarnate Word Academy. Hauling water in times of drought was the job of men called *"barrileros,"* and it was quite a chore, especially in outlying areas of the city. The city's new water system provided assurance of fresh water from the Nueces River and relieved citizens of total dependence on cisterns for their water supply.

These children of the 1894 fifth grade class of the Corpus Christi Public School finished their studies; the next year's students weren't so fortunate. The city spent a great deal of capital on the water supply system, then faced reduced revenue due to the 1893 panic. School funding dropped. Consequently, in 1895, school trustees required payment of a dollar a month for intermediate grades and three dollars for high school, for those who wished to continue their education.

The Corpus Christi Shamrock Hose Company No. 4, shown here around 1900, patrolled the northeastern part of the city. In the first row, from left, are: Joe Mireur, Joe Davidson, Tom Poulson, Charles Lege, and John Gollihar. On the second row are John Davidson, Peyton Smythe, Jim Falvilla, Lucien Young, Willie Young, Clem Vetters, Farrell Benson, Charlie Wilkerson, Tompkins (first name unknown), Max Luther, Bill Gollihar, Wison Rankin, and Joe Dunn. The little girl is Annie Rankin.

This view of Mesquite Street features the H. Keller shop, which sold saddles and saddlery hardware as well as buggies, carriages, and ambulances. This shop was sold to Joe Mireur in 1903. Next to the saddlery is E. Morris' dry goods and clothing store, followed by Norwick Gussett's and El Barego, which bought and sold wool and hides. El Barego also served as a meeting place for vaqueros and traders.

Law enforcement personnel gather on the Hollub Courthouse steps. This 1875 facility designed by Rudolph Hollub replaced the old Nueces County Courthouse (building on left) at Mesquite and Belden streets. The old building was designed by Felix A. Blucher, a surveyor and architect, in 1853. Both buildings were connected by a stairway and deck, and both structures were later replaced by the construction of the 1914 courthouse.

Jailers and residents pose in front of the Nueces County Jail which stood near the Nueces County Courthouse on the 1100 block of Mesquite Street. While the building had fine architecture, it appeared quite bleak because of the desperate prisoners who often peered out its windows, as shown in this picture.

The First Grade class of Miss Ella Thomas stands in front of the Corpus Christi Public School in 1901. Thomas' salary this year was $50.00 per month. The Corpus Christi Public School system had 532 students and 16 teachers that year.

These women are enjoying a popular way to spend the day in the early 1900s. Strolling down the municipal pier and smelling the salt air while talking to friends enticed many to this bay area.

This photograph captures the Corpus Christi High School team in 1904 playing their first football game.

The Epworth Inn had a magnificent view from its North Beach location and attracted many visitors. The Methodist Church of Corpus Christi used the facility to hold summer-long meetings, and because so many followers flocked to the area, the inn rented tents and cots to support the crowd. By 1916, however, the inn canceled these meetings.

This panoramic view of North Beach, where the Methodist Church held summer camp meetings, illustrates the temporary tent cities that drew crowds. With the building of Epworth the amount of tents diminished; however, these camps could still be found near the inn for those who still wished to stay on the beach, or at peak season, for those who could not find rooms at the hotel.

A white Dunne ambulance dashes through town around 1910. Maxwell P. Dunne Funeral Service owned this multipurpose, horse-drawn carriage, which was used as an ambulance and hearse. This business has operated in Corpus Christi since 1908.

This photograph displays the Culpepper home located on Chaparral Street in the early 1900s. Doctor Arthur Spohn used this home as his first hospital. The horse and carriage may be waiting to take the doctor on a house call.

A groom holds a decorated horse and carriage for these two women. The wagon is probably headed for a parade.

The State Hotel located on Star and Mesquite, built by V. M. Donigan in 1907, attracted many visitors to the city. This hotel also housed the Corpus Christi Public Library after the 1919 hurricane destroyed many of the books at its old location in the Hatch and Robertson building. The hotel closed in 1960, and by 1964, the city sought to tear it down.

The sand and surf in front of the Epworth Inn on North Beach provided entertainment for guests. Many of these bathers flocked to this area for the Methodist retreat in the summer. Pleasure boats like the one pictured to the right carried passengers around the bay.

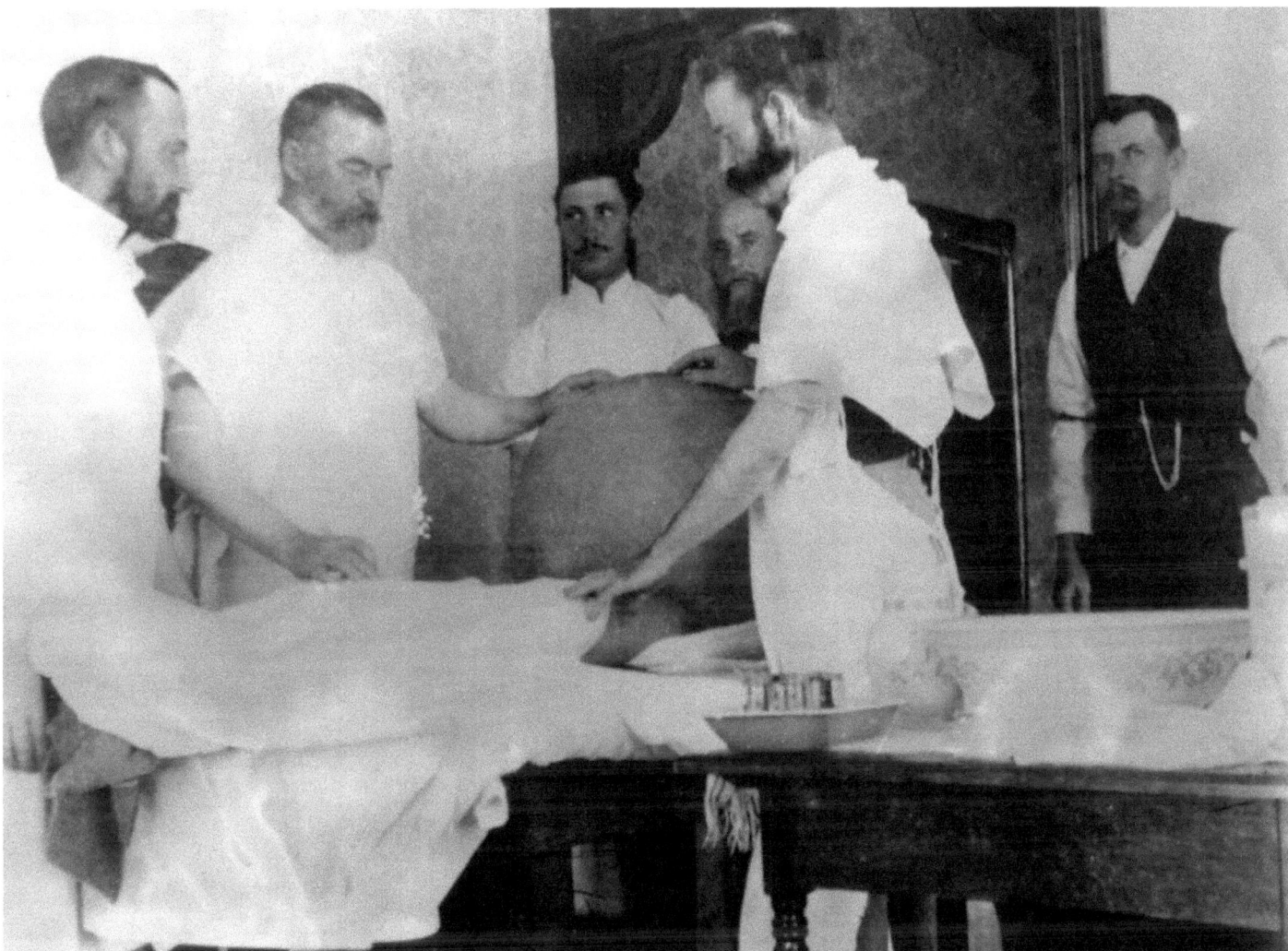

Doctor Arthur E. Spohn (second from the left), along with his assistants, are surveying a patient who has some sort of tumor. Doctor Spohn arrived in Texas in 1868 and later married Sarah Kenedy. He practiced medicine in Corpus Christi until his death in 1913. He was the first president of the Nueces County Medical Association and opened the Spohn Sanitarium on North Beach in 1900.

This is the first official Convent of the Incarnate Word, built in 1886 under Rev. Claude Jaillet. The sisters of the Incarnate Word arrived in Corpus Christi in 1871. They took up residence at the home of Father St. Jean, where they opened a small school. The sisters taught German, French, Spanish, Painting, Drawing, and Sewing. This facility was later built to accommodate the growing number of students.

Employees pose with delivery wagons in front of the Corpus Christi Steam Laundry & Dye Works, located at 112 Mesquite in 1907. The owner, John C. Selvidge, opened this business prior to 1904. By 1915, Mrs. A. B. Selvidge became the owner.

A crowd gathers to view the groundbreaking of a new addition to the west of the city, located on Leopard Street. A lot was to be given out to some lucky resident, which encouraged many to attend.

William Petzel and his nephew, Henry Petzel (left), stand in front of the W. H. Dreyer meat market. Mr. Dreyer boasted he was "the leading butcher and meat man in Corpus Christi." This establishment occupied stalls one and three on the north side of city market, located on Peoples, Schatzel, and Mesquite streets. The building is decorated to welcome firemen for the Firemen's Ball, held upstairs in the ballroom.

Onlookers observe the baptism of several members of the First Baptist Church on July 14, 1907. Reverend D. B. South was pastor of the church at this time. Central Wharf, which provided seating for observers in this picture, washed away during the 1919 storm.

Young Burt Boyd stands in front of Pitts Livery Company, holding a top. In 1905 this business operated as Pitts, Simmons, & Brown Livery and Stable, but by 1908 became Pitts and Baker Livery and Boarding Stable at 310 Mesquite. It provided various services including caring for horses, funeral transportation, and automobile transportation. By 1905 it changed to Fivel and Pitts Garage and Repair Shop, which repaired and sold automobiles.

After a day of hunting just south of town on the Poenish tank in April 1905, these duck hunters hauled their catch to the back of E. H. Caldwells Hardware Store and posed for this picture. The hunters (left to right) are: Frederic Louis Magnenat, Robert Hall, Lawrence Grimage, John Biggio, Sam Anderson, and Joe Downey.

These two women stroll down Central Wharf on March 3, 1908, carrying their catch for the day. Central Wharf, located between Williams and Laguna streets, had many functions. It was used to load cattle and other cargo onto ships, provided good access for fishermen, and by 1903, had a bathhouse that supplied fresh water for showers.

This slide, "Old Nat," near Twigg Street and the Natorium Bathhouse, supplied ample fun for residents as well as visitors. The windmill drew water from the bay and poured it down the slide to add momentum and speed for these enthusiasts.

A horse and wagon loaded with lumber are ready to make a delivery from the E. D. Sidbury business located at 222 Chaparral Street in 1908. This lumber company specialized in pine and cypress lumber. They also made shingles, doors, blinds, moldings, stairs, and balusters.

The November 17, 1908, Inland Waterway Convention drew crowds, as this view of the front of the Salt Cedar Garden at the Seaside Hotel illustrates. The distinguished gentleman leaning on his cane in the center of the photograph is William Jennings Bryan. He had lost his bid for the presidency once again, so he escaped to Corpus Christi to relax at the home of Mrs. G. R. Scott.

Sunbathing and swimming has enticed visitors as well as residents to North Beach since the end of the nineteenth century. These young women sharing the joys of their youth in their stylish 1909 beachwear are a sample of the tourists who congregated in this area. In the background are the wood-framed tourist cabins of Ring Villa, built by F. E. Ring. They did not survive the 1919 hurricane.

This scene focuses on the streetcar tracks running down Chaparral Street. Peter Herdic brought the first streetcars to Corpus Christi in 1880, mule-drawn coaches that seated ten passengers. Steam-powered streetcars replaced these "Herdies" in 1890. Many residents and tourists rode these cars to go shopping or out to the Alta Vista Hotel to walk along the beach.

This electric trolley drew a crowd when the first car approached its stop in March of 1910. Daniel Hewitt, proprietor, ran a loop through the city to North Beach. At a nickel a ride, passengers traveled around town at a speed of 10 to 15 miles an hour. In 1911 the company experienced financial difficulties and was sold to the Heinley Brothers of Denver, which operated as the Corpus Christi Street and Interurban Railway Company.

This majestic North Beach structure, called Corpus Beach Hotel or the Breakers Hotel, catered to Corpus Christi's increasing number of tourists in 1912. During World War I it was transformed to become the U.S. Public Health convalescent hospital. A year after war's end, the 1919 hurricane slammed into the building, severely damaging it. After years of neglect, the hotel was restored, only to be destroyed by Hurricane Celia in 1970.

Several of the bystanders who observed the remains of a 1916 White Point gas well blowout are (left to right) Annie Piehl, Minnie Freier, Paul Freier (baby), and L. J. Piehl. Debris and pipe are all that are left of the derrick.

This post–1910 view of downtown Corpus Christi illustrates the progress that occurred in this city during that time. The trolley system and roads are developed, and many houses and businesses now dot the area. On the left is the Corpus Christi National Bank. Farther down the street, the building with the tall peak is the Church of the Good Shepherd.

This is the Cahill Plumbing Company, located in the Coleman Building at the corner of Mesquite and Starr streets. During the second decade of the twentieth century, when this picture was taken, Corpus Christi only had three plumbing businesses listed in the city directory.

The 1910 Corpus Christi High School football team poses in front of the bleachers on the football field.

In 1912, a group of men stand in front of one of the first planes to land on Corpus Christi's beach. The Pavillion Hotel Pier, in the background to the left, extended from Taylor Street.

After experiencing mechanical difficulties, this plane landed on North Beach in 1913. The men from left to right are: Charles de Remer, W. G. Blake, E. G. Crabbe, and Eli Merriman. Remer, the pilot, was attempting to deliver mail to Port Aransas, but since he could not make the trip, it was sent by boat.

The tables are awaiting guests in the dining room of the Alta Vista Hotel, but this establishment never really opened. Elihu Harrison Ropes began construction, and in 1891 the unfinished hotel hosted a ball, but the 1893 panic eliminated funds for its completion. New owner J. J. Copley purchased the building in 1905 and furnished the hotel, but abandoned the building in 1912. In 1927, fire destroyed the structure.

This photo features members of the city's 1914 police department. From left to right are: Pat Feely, Ike Johnson, Willie Petzel, Ed Nycum, Lee Petzel, Chief Claude Fowler, John White, Doc Scogin, J. W. Priestly, O. B. Prather, and Glen McCauly.

This picture of the bluff focuses on the Pompeo Coppini sculpture and the steps leading up the hill toward the Presbyterian Church, around 1914. This art sculpture features a woman in the center, which represents Corpus Christi, receiving blessings from Mother Earth and Father Neptune. The Presbyterian Church behind the sculpture was completed in 1901 and provided services until 1929, when the building was sold.

A railroad clerk sits at his desk and a passenger awaits her train in this photograph taken in August of 1911. Corpus Christi had three depots, the San Antonio Aransas Pass, Texas Mexican, and the Union. This is probably the ticket office for the San Antonio Aransas Pass, later known as the Southern Pacific Railroad.

The Draughons College of Corpus Christi was part of a chain of business colleges that sprouted throughout the United States because of the efforts of Professor John F. Draughon. He began these institutions in 1879 and in Corpus Christi advertised the teaching of Spelling, Machine Bookkeeping, Comptometer, Cotton Spanish Business Administration, Salesmanship, Higher Accounting, Business English, Shorthand, Typewriting, Bookeeping, Accounting, Correspondence, Filing, Penmanship, Business Arithmetic, and Commercial Law.

A streetcar makes a stop on Chaparral Street around 1910 to pick up passengers.

Clerks sitting at their desks around 1910 at the Corpus Christi Transfer Company, which sold tickets for the San Antonio & Aransas Pass Railroad Company (S.A.A.P.), located at 614 Chaparral Street. This line would merge and change its name, and finally link this area with the Louisville & Nashville line.

The Horne Apartments in the early 1900s were located at 716 Chaparral. A resident peers into the street, while a woman sits on the balcony reading. Mrs. Helen R. Horne operated the apartments in 1899. Forty-seven years later, in 1946, she decided to close, because at age 75 she wanted to retire.

The 1914 Nueces County Courthouse is a wonderful example of classical design. Architect Harvey L. Page designed the building, and construction began in 1914. The following year, residents invited to view the spectacular building witnessed its opulence and modern courtrooms. This well-built jewel protected many residents during the devastation of the 1919 hurricane, but after 64 years the building was abandoned and has been left in disrepair.

Automobiles park on either side of the Nueces Hotel. Built in 1913, and located on Water and Peoples streets, the building had a wonderful bay view. Tourists and residents alike flocked to this elegant hotel, and many business meetings were conducted in its dining room and on its sun porch. The building received damage from Hurricane Celia in 1970 and was torn down the following year.

The Seaside Pavilion Hotel built by Jack Ennis rested on Taylor Street, overlooking the bay. Visitors congregated in the cool breezes under the shade of the salt cedars. Tourists enjoyed the hotel's many amenities, including the excellent meals served in the dining room. Swimmers and fisherman also appreciated Corpus Christi's natural view from the pier. The building and pier were destroyed by the 1919 hurricane.

The 1916 hurricane caused severe damage to the Corpus Christi Gulf and Country Club, located on North Beach at Water and Elm streets. This building hosted several notable individuals including President William Howard Taft, who dedicated the building in 1909. Although the building sustained major damage in the 1916 hurricane, it would take the 1919 hurricane to finally claim the building.

The Hardin Court Grocery located at 1801 North Water Street experienced major damage from the hurricane that hit Corpus Christi in August of 1916. Mounds of debris in front of the building made clean-up a chore.

After reading an article in the 1910 *Saturday Evening Post* about the Sea Scouts and their ability to build character in young boys, a Mrs. Furman thought Corpus Christi should have a troop. In 1911, Troop 1 formed with Thomas Allen as their leader (holding flag), and the boys (from left) Robert Meitzer, Wade Mount, Coulter McCusition, and Frank Austin. Troop 2 formed shortly after with Oliver S. Caldwell as its leader.

U. S. Heinley sits at the front of this electric trolley in 1914. This trolley belonged to the Corpus Christi Street and Interurban Railway Co., which the Heinley Brothers bought in 1911 from Daniel Hewitt. This enterprise eventually expanded city routes and added three new cars to their fleet. In 1919 the hurricane destroyed most of the track, which was later repaired and operated by the company until 1931.

Charles A. Meuly , Ursula Marie Magnerat, and Frances Magnerat stand next to their automobile in front of their home on Blucher and Carrizo streets. Charles Meuly was the son of Conrad Meuly, who arrived in Corpus Christi in 1850. He was a survivor of the Mier Expedition, a raiding party captured by the Mexican Army on Christmas Day, 1842. The men were forced to draw beans to see who would be executed. Conrad Meuly was among the lucky ones who drew a white bean instead of a black one.

This photograph taken from the bluff, looking down Williams Street, illustrates the damage the downtown area suffered from the 1919 hurricane. Debris lines the streets, many homes are missing, and others are unstable because of the excessive wind and rising water that pummeled the city.

This photograph, taken five days after the surprise hurricane of 1919, exposes the havoc the storm wreaked on the city. W. E. Breman (white shirt center) stands in the middle of Laguna Street peering at the wreckage while men on Mesquite Street load lumber onto a truck. An electric trolley sits idle in the aftermath of one of the worst hurricanes ever to hit Corpus Christi.

The massive debris of crushed wood and metal littered Water Street, and salvage workers had a difficult time clearing the area. The National Guard arrived in Corpus Christi to aid in restoring order and help with the cleanup.

Several men are seen walking amidst the debris left by the storm surge of the 1919 hurricane, searching for the deceased. This storm claimed an unknown number of lives; many victims were never found. A stone monument in Rose Hill Cemetery commemorates those lost in this storm.

After the 1919 hurricane most of North Beach, devoid of houses and buildings, attracted residents back to its shores to enjoy the sand and surf. This picture taken in 1922 shows men and women on a merry-go-round, having fun on the beach.

Constructed in 1871 on the corner of Chaparral and Taylor streets, the Episcopal Church of the Good Shepherd withstood the 1919 hurricane but was severely damaged. The church expanded and moved to this new location. Members also commissioned a statue of a shepherd, which was designed by resident and surgeon Sherman T. Coleman, to be placed near the building.

This 1920s automobile travels through the intersection of Mesquite and Lawrence streets.
The prominent building in the photograph is the Bidwell Hotel, formerly known as the
Constantine Hotel in the first decade of the twentieth century. The building was turned into a
furniture store in 1940 by Albert Lichtenstein and was torn down in 1999.

Students and their teachers pose in front of the Incarnate Word Academy. The Sisters of the Incarnate Word and Blessed Sacrament arrived in Corpus Christi in 1871. They soon bought property surrounded by Leopard, Carancahua, Antelope, and Tancahua streets where they constructed the building seen here. This building would be moved in 1926 to make room for a bigger brick structure to accommodate the growing student population.

Mesquite Street at Schatzel was bustling in the 1920s. Residents brought their children with them to shop along this thoroughfare. The building to the right is the First State Bank, designed by Mayor Dan Reid in 1908. The bank changed ownership several times, and by 1922 it was known as State National Bank, which merged with Corpus Christi National Bank in 1956.

Pedestrians walk along Chaparral in front of the Simon-Cohn Co. department store, which opened by 1924 and operated for at least the next ten years. To the left of this building is the Kress Five and Dime Store, which opened in 1916 and weathered several big storms and hurricanes. This stable city fixture closed its doors 75 years later in 1991.

Automobiles are parked on both sides of the Meehans Dry Goods Co. store. The business operated out of this location at 515 Chaparral in the Uehlinger Building from at least 1924 to 1932.

The Making of a Modern City

(1926–1939)

By 1926 the city was on the path to recovery from the 1919 hurricane. The *John Jacobson* and *Matagorda* finished deepening the channel and, on September 14, the city celebrated the opening of the port. A parade by military and civilians alike marched in the middle of town. Representatives of the federal, state, and local governments gave speeches and, along with the Navigation Commission, opened the festivities. Pedestrians later lined the dock to witness the first ship, the USS *Borie,* travel under the Bascule Bridge with Governor Pat Neff and Mayor P. G. Lovenskiold on deck, which signified the opening of the port. Boat races and a beauty contest followed the opening, while several dozen bands played throughout the day. With the beauty contestant chosen, a skit of the city's history from 1519 to 1926 was performed for the meandering crowds, extending the celebration into the evening. The joining of hands between King Neptune and Miss Corpus Christi implied the opening of the port and the end of the play. A massive fireworks display followed, ending the festivities.

The port is significant because it was the catalyst which transformed and propelled the city toward modernity. By 1930 the population doubled and the city's tallest buildings—the Nixon, Driscoll, and Plaza—jutted toward the sky. With the coming of the Great Depression business expansion decreased, but the city actually escaped the worst effects of this era. While the scarcity of jobs took its toll on many communities, Corpus Christi actually advertised for office workers, skilled mechanics, and construction workers to supply the Southern Alkali Company, a new business located along the port, which used oyster shells to produce chlorine and soda ash. This enterprise required additional improvements to the port, and these modifications encouraged other industries to locate along the channel.

The discovery of oil and gas in the area also offset the depression by attracting workers for exploration and later for construction of chemical and refinery plants. The county's cotton production also led the nation in 1930, and other agricultural and consumer goods passed through the port, making Corpus Christi one of the major cities in Texas.

Three destroyers, the USS *Hatfield, John D. Edwards,* and *Borie,* decorated to celebrate the opening of the port on September 14, 1926. Pedestrians crowd along the dock to witness this historic event and catch a glimpse of Governor Pat Neff and Mayor P. G. Lovenskiold. The port would soon bring a booming commerce to the area and forever transform the city's skyline.

The Bascule Bridge stands fully open to allow the destroyer USS *Borie* to travel through to the newly opened port. The Bascule Bridge (which means seesaw), built over Hall's Bayou (now the ship channel), opened six weeks prior to the opening of the port. This $400,000 investment was hailed as the "Pride of South Texas." The bridge was retired in 1959, after 33 years of service. *Borie* went on to win a Presidential Unit Citation and four battle stars during World War II.

A little girl waits in this fancy 1920s automobile, with clean, white-walled tires, parked in front of the W. W. Jones building at 511 South Broadway. The home was built in 1905, and Jones and his family lived there until 1938. The city also used this building from 1935 to 1955 as a library.

Florence Kaler (bookkeeper) and Freda Kaler (stenographer) stand behind the counter, surrounded by lights, lamps, and other fixtures adorning the inside of the Smith Electric Company. The building located at 619 Mesquite opened for business around 1926 and operated at this location until 1939.

The delivery cars parked along Leopard Street in front of the South Texas Candy Co. are waiting to deliver their goods. This business, established around 1928, produced several different sweets for the growing Corpus Christi area.

Employees stand outside the Nueces Coffee Co. at 707 Lester in this image. The business was established in 1929 with Sam Beilin as president, W. E. Bivens as vice-president, and Sam Charles as secretary-treasurer.

Automobiles are lined up for a B. F. Goodrich promotion outside the Texas Motor Sales Co. in 1929.

The well-stocked Acme Concrete Pipe Company, operated by Russel Lyons & Carl Henny at 501 Doss, provided pipe and other fixtures to the growing city in 1935.

This vehicle travels down the "S" curve from Upper Broadway to Lower Broadway just north of Twigg Street in the 1930s. The tallest building in the background is the Nueces Building. The parked car on the left is in front of what will become the site of the Caller-Times building, constructed in 1935.

Pedestrians lounge, looking at the bay from Pleasure Pier. This view of the pier has the downtown area in the background with the Pier Café, owned by John Govatos, on the left. The café opened in 1926 in an old wooden building, but in 1932 the restaurant moved to this location and remained open until 1942.

The Borden Company was operating in Corpus Christi by 1933, with J. M. Conoly as manager.
Located on the corner of Waco and Blucher streets, it was one of two milk processing plants in the city.
The other was Hygeia, which operated in conjunction with Knolle Farms.

This was the 1934 office of the Southern Pacific Railway freight station located on Belden and Power streets. The clerks in the picture are identified, left to right, as: George Gould (agent), Jimmy Brooks (chief clerk), Ed Beasley (telegrapher), Dick Leahy (yard clerk), Deacon Saunders (clerk), D. R. Prince (round house), A. Patrick (assistant agent), and Jack Cheaney (rate clerk).

This photograph of the Nueces Hardware Co., located at 323 Chaparral Street, was taken in 1935. The business had operated at this location since at least 1927.

Fishing, a popular pastime for many who venture to the breakwaters along the bay front, enticed tourists and locals alike in 1935. Since the devastation of the 1919 hurricane, the city embarked on a plan to protect its urban area, which led to the construction of this concrete barrier. The breakwaters, completed in 1925, protect the city from massive surges, and the jetties provide residents with a place to fish and relax.

This photograph illustrates the bayfront improvement project in action with a view of the intersection of Peoples and Water streets. Automobiles travel on the newly cleaned beach in front of the Nueces Hotel. The building to the left is the Medical-Professional Building, and the tall building on the bluff is the Robert Driscoll Hotel.

North Beach in the 1930s became a center where many gathered to meet friends, swim, and generally enjoy the weekend.

Corpus Christi at this time had several hotels and restaurants that catered to businessmen. These patrons are enjoying their lunch at an unidentified restaurant.

Guests enjoy the opulence of the Nueces Hotel's Tropical Garden dining room. Tourists and residents enjoyed the relaxing atmosphere and good food. Many business meetings and parties took place in this room.

A class in 1936 poses along with Coach Tom Quigby (bottom far right) in front of the Corpus Christi Academy.

Automobiles line both sides of Upper Broadway in this 1937 photograph. In the background, the Plaza Hotel stands to the right. This 14-story hotel, which towered over the other buildings on the bluff, was later replaced with an even taller structure, the 600 Building.

This picture documents the 45 members of the Corpus Christi Kiwanis Club who traveled to Austin for a meeting in 1936.

This four-story building, opened by Clark Pease on Chaparral and Peoples streets, is the City National Bank. Pease arrived in Corpus Christi in 1904 and opened a small bank, but soon after merged with a national entity to form the City National Bank. The bank operated at this location until 1938, when the Corpus Christi National Bank moved to this area.

Pedestrians and their dogs stroll down Pleasure Pier, enjoying the weather.

Bishop Ledvina, assisted by Bishop Garriga and Monsignor Lannon, led the groundbreaking ceremony for the new St. Patrick's Cathedral in 1939. The church was later dedicated as the Corpus Christ Cathedral, in 1940.

Residents enjoy fishing from the jetties on a beautiful October day in 1939.

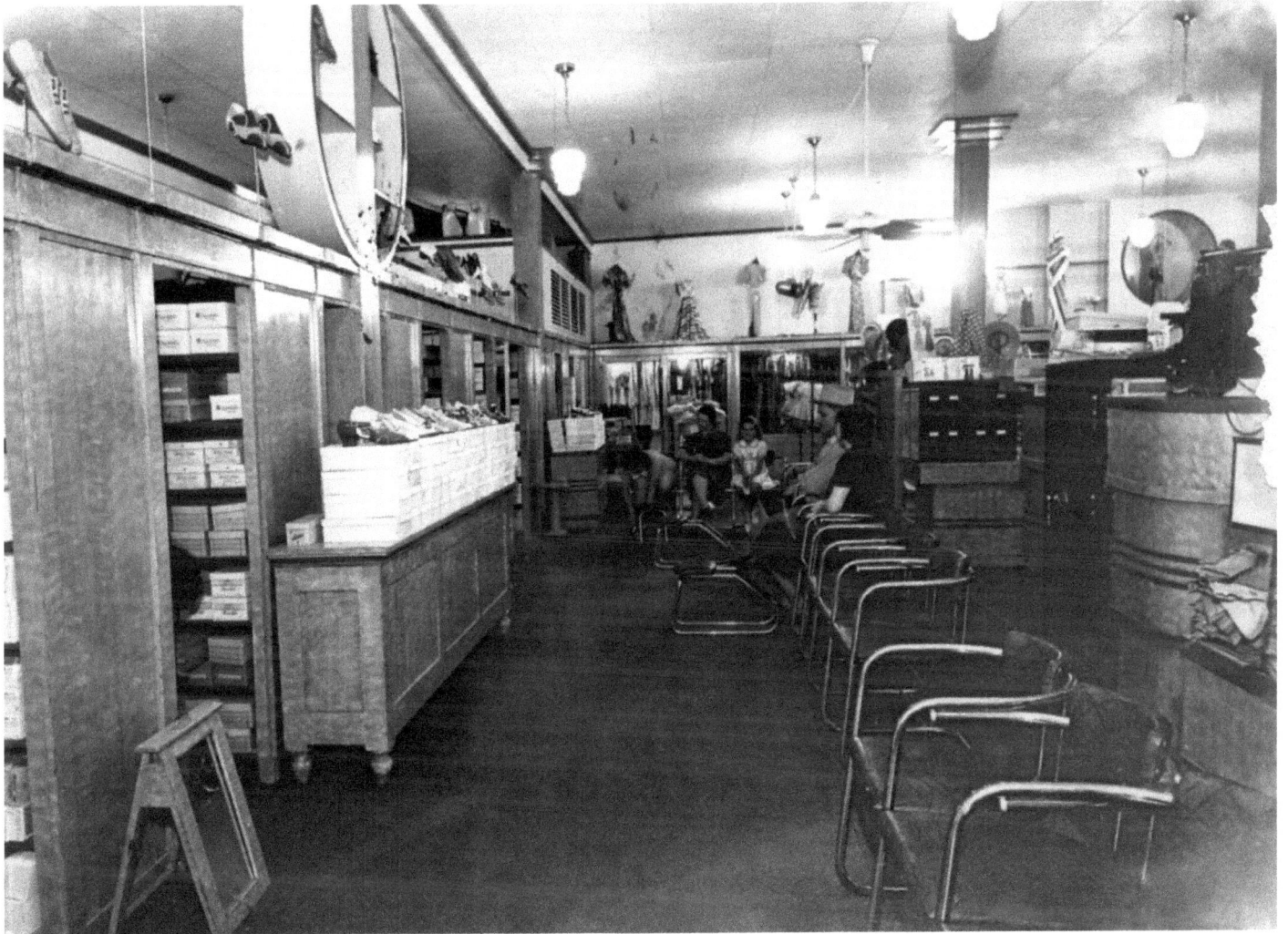

In 1939, when this photograph was taken, Corpus Christi had at least ten different shoe stores and twenty shops to repair shoes.

This is a festive view of Chaparral Street with numerous cars and holiday shoppers. On the left a line of house trailers extends for blocks. On the right is the Lichtenstein building. The dominating structure on the right is the Medical-Professional Building. Across Peoples Street is the Nueces Hotel and barely visible is the Palace Theater.

War Years and Aftermath

(1940–1949)

The continued growth of the previous decade spilled over into this era for Corpus Christi. The city now had a variety of industries, including Southern Oil and Refining, Taylor Refining, and Columbia Carbon. Pontiac Refinery opened in 1941, followed by American Smelting and Refining and Sinclair Refinery the next year. The exploration for oil and gas continued during this decade, although it slowed somewhat during the critical years of the war. With the addition of these industries, the city also expanded its services, including the building of a 12,000-foot-long seawall, which forever changed the landscape of downtown. This structure added protection and provided a wonderful place to sit and enjoy the bay view.

Another boon for the city at this time was the creation of the Naval Air Station. President Franklin Delano Roosevelt signed an appropriation of funds for this facility, and the following year, on March 12, 1941, the base was officially dedicated. The station was originally used as a training facility for aviation cadets, pilots, gunners, radio operators, and aerologists. The main station, located in Flour Bluff, along with four auxiliary stations in Corpus Christi (Rodd, Cuddihy, Cabaniss, and Waldron), required many construction workers and other key personnel. By 1944, over 40,000 civilians worked at these stations, and the influx of these workers, as well as military personnel, caused a housing shortage. Many families were forced to camp on the beach or take whatever housing they could find. The station spurred a housing boom, as well as the expansion of businesses that provided consumer goods. Entertainment venues such as clubs, movie theaters, and carnivals opened all over the city to provide this transient population with amusements. At war's end, the Naval Air Station cut back its workforce, but the facility still served as a training center and added a few other services, including the precision fliers, the Blue Angels.

This decade saw the city again double in population, because many who found employment here decided to stay. The natural beauty coupled with the growth potential from the port and other industries enticed visitors to call this city home.

Corpus Christi received several new government offices with the coming of the Naval Air Station, such as this United States Engineering Field Office.

The 1941 Buccaneer Days Parade featured the ROTC marching down the bluff to Lower Broadway. This parade had its origins in celebrating Spanish explorer and mapmaker Alonso Alvarez de Pineda's visit to the area in 1519 as part of his assigned task of mapping the Gulf Coast from Florida to Mexico for the governor of Jamaica. The first parade, held on June 3, 1938, featured a Spanish galleon anchored to the breakwater and a discovery reenactment of Pineda's first step onshore. This event has been a major attraction in the city since its debut.

This drive-in sandwich shop built near the construction site of the Naval Air Station fed many of the construction workers, as well as those employed at the base.

With the influx of new residents to the area, many lived in these "shotgun" houses, so called because it was said a shotgun could fire through the back door from the front door and not hit anything in between. The ease of construction provided shelter for many in this area. This photograph is probably of a father and his two sons.

After a long evening that involved drinks stronger than Coca-Cola at a North Beach "honky-tonk," these men decided to take a nap on the beach.

This view of Chaparral Street illustrates the vast number of automobiles that have been acquired by residents of the town. The building on the right in the foreground is Draughons Practical Business College. Many women attended this school to learn clerical skills, which allowed them to take advantage of the new employment opportunities being created in the Corpus Christi area.

The Corpus Christi High School Buccaneer football team poses in front of the goal posts in 1941.

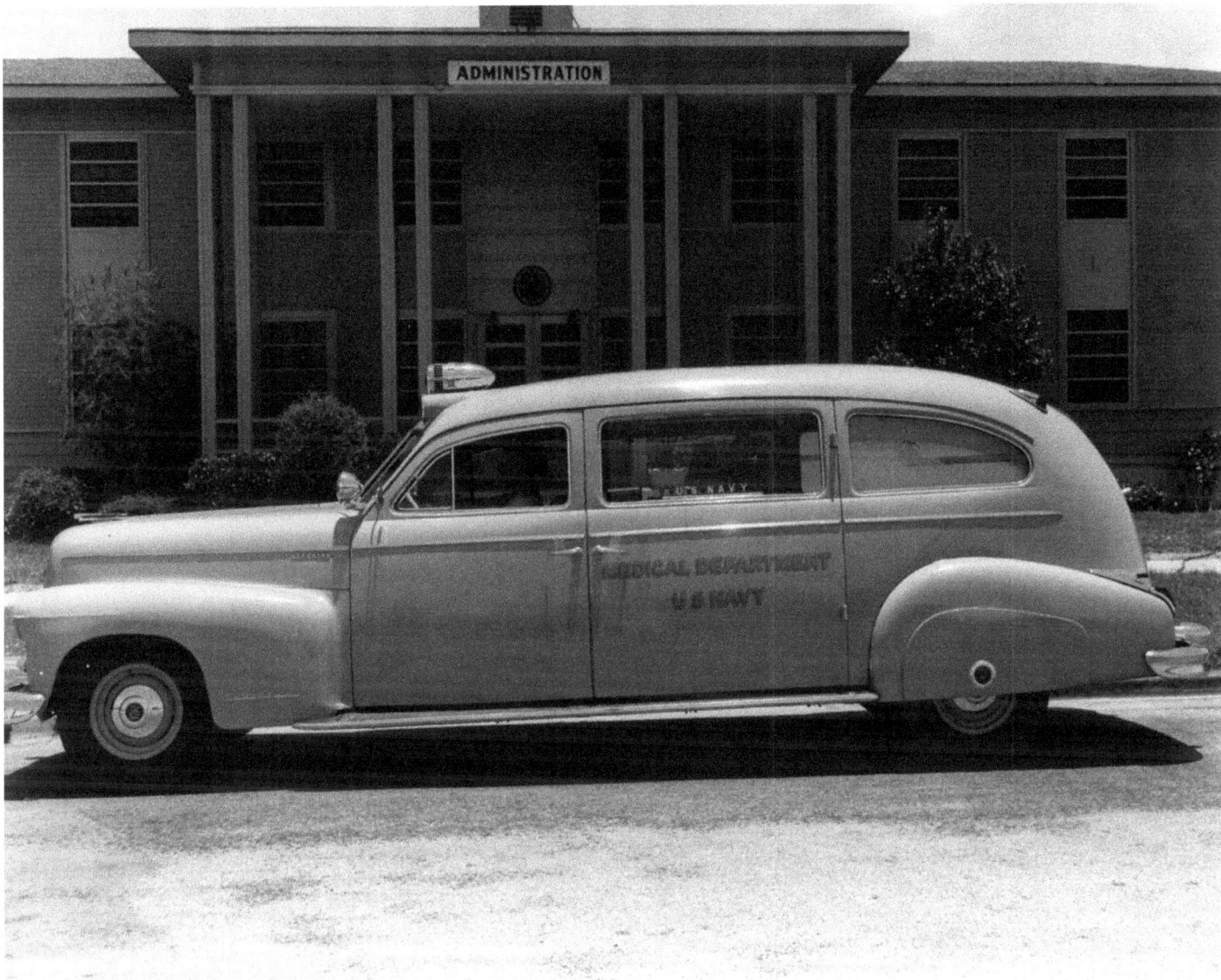

This United States Navy Medical Department ambulance is parked in front of the Administration Building at the Naval Air Station. Construction for the Administration Building began in 1940. It was the first structure completed on the base.

This wooden building housed the Southern Paint Supply business at 1602 Ayers, managed by
Mack Hood. The company sold various paints and supplies, including tools and household items.

Several automobiles are parked in front of the U.S. Post Office and Custom House, located on Antelope and North Upper Broadway. Groundbreaking ceremonies for this building took place on November 12, 1938, with Congressman Richard M. Kleberg, Sr., as speaker. The building was completed the following year and opened on September 1, 1939.

The Lighthouse Café at 1422 North Water Street was a popular eatery in 1942. The structure's entrance replicated a lighthouse with a beacon at the top of the tower.

This photograph pictures a Navy advertisement taken right after Christmas in 1941. Since the coming of the Naval Air Station to Corpus Christi, the community has strongly supported this segment of the armed services.

Drug store soda fountains, like this one photographed in 1943, served all kinds of treats, ranging from coffee and sandwiches to ice cream and other delicacies. They were popular social meeting places for both youths and adults in Corpus Christi.

This amusement park on North Beach in 1942 drew crowds, especially the servicemen from the Naval Air Station, to ride the Tilt-A-Whirl, carousal, Ferris wheel, and the like. If the rides weren't enough fun, visitors could go for a swim and dive into the saltwater pool. Crowds were especially numerous during holidays and special events such as air shows, beauty contests, and boat shows.

A pilot stands beside his plane.

Pilots and their instructors pose in front of a fleet of U.S. Navy airplanes at the Naval Air Station. Two-seater biplanes like these were generally used for training purposes in World War II.

The WAVES are enjoying some cake with their commanding officer.

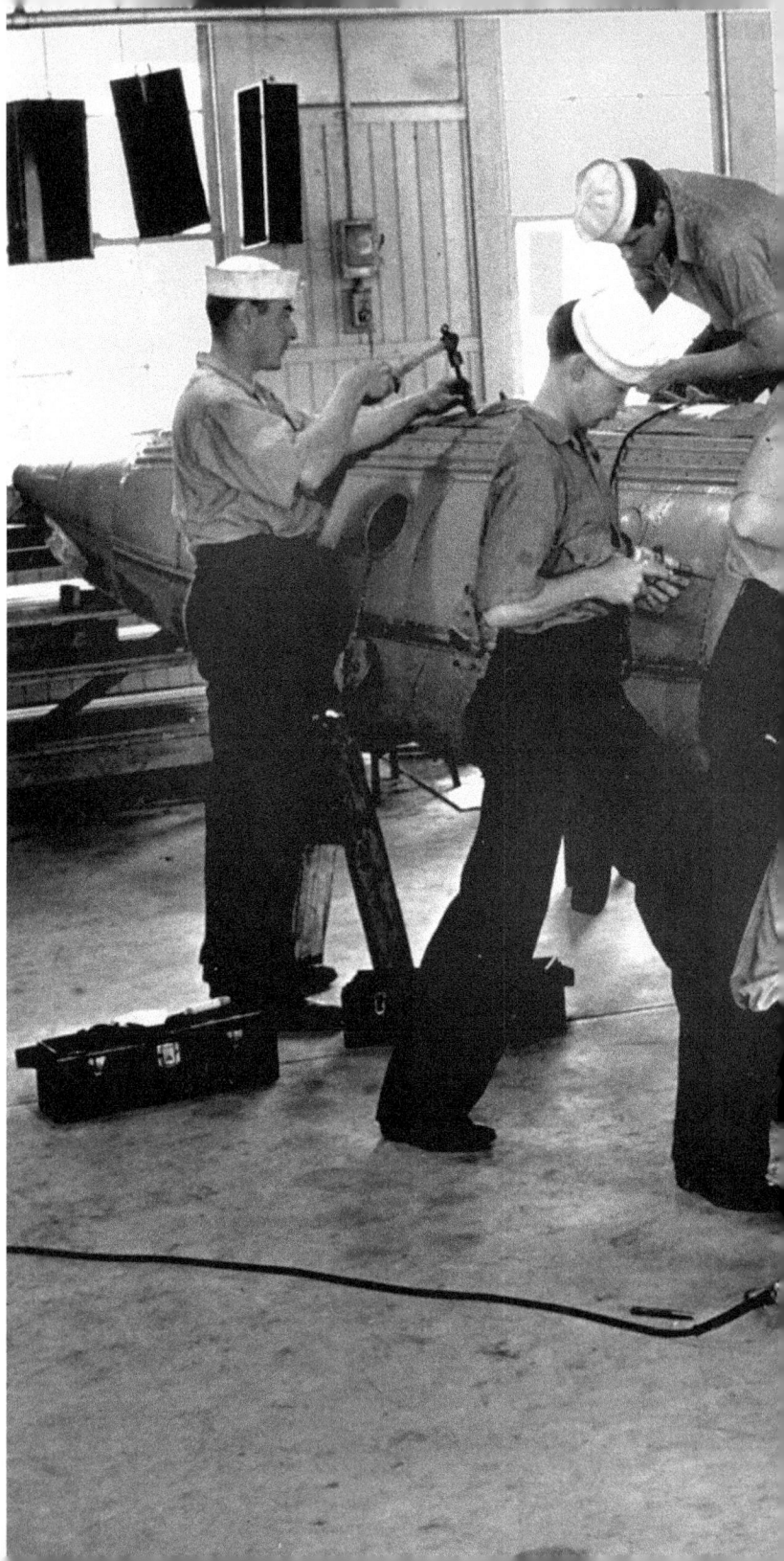

Navy personnel build a plane under the watchful eye of
an officer at the Naval Air Station.

This view of the city taken from the bluff illustrates the rapid growth of buildings during the 1940s.

Sailors and civilians alike relaxed and enjoyed themselves in the many clubs that popped up in town during the war years.

El Patio Mexican Food restaurant at 201 North Water advertised fine and unique Mexican food.

Volunteer women of the Red Cross in 1944 helped the war effort by making first aid kits, knitting scarves, gloves and socks, and sewing various garments for men and women in the armed services. During this time the organization also attracted nurses to teach first aid to the police department and to civilians. They also worked at the naval hospital and helped many during the hurricane of 1942.

Servicemen listen to Lieutenant Ronnie Durham, a member of the Civil Air Patrol,
explain how to use the radio telephone equipment.

Corpus Christi during the war years had a large transient population because of the Naval Air Base. Entertainment arenas sprang up all over the city, including theaters, dance halls, and clubs.

A Navy band from the Naval Air Station entertains a crowd in 1944.

Corpus Christi fireman John Carlisle, Watt Cooper, and A. O. Gibson demonstrate lifesaving practices to other members of the fire department. Victor Garrott volunteered to be the "victim" for this demonstration.

This view of Upper Broadway to the north highlights the city's tallest buildings in the 1940s. In the foreground is the Nixon Building. Across the street is the Plaza Hotel, and next to it is the Driscoll Hotel.

The Naval Air Station undergoes an inspection on June 18, 1946, with Admiral C. W. Nimitz presiding. Mayor Robert Wilson, Tom Graham, and Admiral Jocko Clark join Nimitz on stage for the ceremonies.

Doctor Edward L. Harvin, president of Del Mar College for two decades, works at his desk. An American history teacher, Harvin assumed the role as president of this junior college in 1946. Under his leadership, Del Mar evolved into one of the leading junior colleges in the state. After retiring, Harvin returned to the classroom and taught American history for another two years.

The main section of the Church of the Good Shepherd is being moved from Upper Broadway and Park to its new location on Staples Street in 1949. This Episcopal Church, one of the oldest churches in the city, was organized in 1874. Two years later, New York architect Richard Upjohn built this Gothic structure on the corner of Chaparral and Taylor. In the background is the First Presbyterian Church.

CAMP FIRE
78
GIRLS

The Camp Fire Girls along with their leader stand beside a Corpus Christi ambulance. The Camp Fire Girls, founded in 1910 in Vermont by Luther Gulick, M.D., and Charlotte Gulick, quickly spread throughout the United States. By 1912 the organization was incorporated, and many major cities including Corpus Christi would have a club.

The Blue Angels fly over the bay with the Corpus Christi skyline in the background in 1949. These Navy planes entertain the public with their flying skills and intricate aerial maneuvers.

Hector P. Garcia stands in front of the American G. I. Forum flag. This organization, originally formed to protect Mexican American veterans' rights, began in Corpus Christi in 1948, with Garcia as chairman. By 1949 it became a statewide organization and soon expanded its scope to fight discrimination wherever it was found.

Automobiles line up in front of the North Gate Sentry House at the Naval Air Station. Private First Class N. J. Dyess with the United States Marine Corps salutes the first visitor onto the Naval Air Station for an Armed Forces Day celebration.

The Growing Metropolis

(1950–1969)

At the dawning of the 1950s, Corpus Christi entered the Cold War era on an upward course. The city built its largest recreational facility, the Memorial Coliseum, which accommodated concerts, shows, and conventions. The dome-shaped building, a memorial to fallen servicemen of World War II, became a noted feature of the bayfront.

The Naval Air Station continued its operations until 1959, when the repair facility of the station closed, causing the loss of over 3,000 jobs. Two years later, however, the helicopter repair service moved to the Naval Air Station, and many people found work again. The escalation of the Vietnam War caused the Naval Air Station to expand and subsequently brought more people to the area.

The port also continued to flourish, and the shipment of cotton and grains continued to expand. In 1952, a 2-million-bushel grain elevator was built along the channel to handle storage, and a few years later additional elevators would double this capacity. By 1969, the port of Corpus Christi was the second-largest in the state. Agricultural shipments of cotton also continued to grow, as well as the shipment of crude petroleum, fuel oils, gasoline, and natural gas. The increase of refineries in the area made this city a major petrochemical center. To make exportation more profitable, and to accommodate larger ships, the Harbor Bridge was built, completed by 1959.

Tourism also escalated during the 1950s and 1960s. Boating enticed many to the bay, and fisherman took advantage of the T-heads, seawall, or public piers and jetties. Automobiles became prevalent. Many drivers loved to cruise around, viewing the city's natural beauty. The newly built Island Causeway (JFK Causeway), which opened in 1950, became a popular destination. This strip of land provided the city with a convenient way to visit Padre Island. When the causeway opened, over 4,500 cars drove through the toll in less than two days. Padre Island drew tourists to the area and many celebrated the holidays, weekends, or summer vacations there.

By 1968, the population reached over 200,000. The city would continue to grow for decades to come. Kinney's seaport town and Rope's vision of Corpus Christi during the second half of the nineteenth century had finally come to fruition a century later.

This view of the 1950s bluff features numerous automobiles parked on Lower Broadway. The tall buildings on the hill are the Driscoll Hotel, Plaza Hotel, and the Nixon Building across the street.

THIS DINING ROOM CAN BE RESERVED FOR
8 TO 35 PEOPLE ANY DAY EXCEPT
Saturday Sunday & Holidays

A group of people gather for a dining-room celebration at Corpus Christi Junior College, also known as Del Mar College. This upper-level institution, organized in 1935, filled a need among the city's growing population. Military personnel were invited to attend classes at the same cost as residents, providing opportunities for many to further their education goals.

This photograph of the La Retama Public Library Bookmobile was taken in September 1951. The bookmobile contained shelves with awnings that opened and closed for ease of access as well as travel. This vehicle brought library services to the public and later had a regular school route. The building to the front of the vehicle is the W. W. Jones home, which housed the library until 1955.

The W. W. Jones house located at 511 South Upper Broadway was built in 1905 and served as Jones' residence until his death. The building was purchased in 1937 to house the library. The La Retama Public Library remained at this location for 18 years, but in 1955 the library moved into a larger and more modern facility (old city hall) at the corner of Mesquite and Peoples streets.

Joe J. Alsup stops to pose in front of the John A. Ferris Men's Wear shop at 611 Leopard as he campaigns on his bannered bicycle for the position of district attorney.

The Corpus Christi Trust Company opened in 1928 on Schatzel Street, and the following year it moved up the hill and changed its name to the Corpus Christi Bank and Trust. The bank continued to expand and purchased this building located on Leopard and Tancahua streets, formerly owned by Perkins Brothers Department Store. The bank remained at this location until 1982 when it moved to the Bank and Trust Plaza.

Employees of the Corpus Christi Bank and Trust Company pose during their Christmas party on December 16, 1954.

First Baptist Church opened on March 26, 1950, at 3115 Ocean Drive with Dr. C. E. Hereford as pastor. The building had an auditorium for 1,200 and an educational building with classrooms. The building was later enlarged in 1967 with a new addition containing a sanctuary and an elevated amphitheater. The original church, formed in 1878, was one of the oldest churches in the area.

A crowd gathers on the platform where the *Inger* docks at a wharf in the Corpus Christi ship channel.

Students dance the night away at a Del Mar College affair.

Construction is underway for the Harbor Bridge in 1956. This new structure would take the place of the 1926 Bascule Bridge, which could not accommodate larger ships entering the port because of its limited 97-foot-wide opening. The Harbor Bridge construction, completed on October 23, 1959, allowed vehicles to cross the ship channel with ease and added a new feature to the bayfront view.

The Nueces Hotel at 308 Peoples Street was still a very popular hotel during the 1950s. Its opulence transcended time, and local businessmen, civic organizations, and other clubs and residents used this facility for a meeting place.

Lou Turbeville and an unidentified driver race their vehicles around a track in the 1950s.

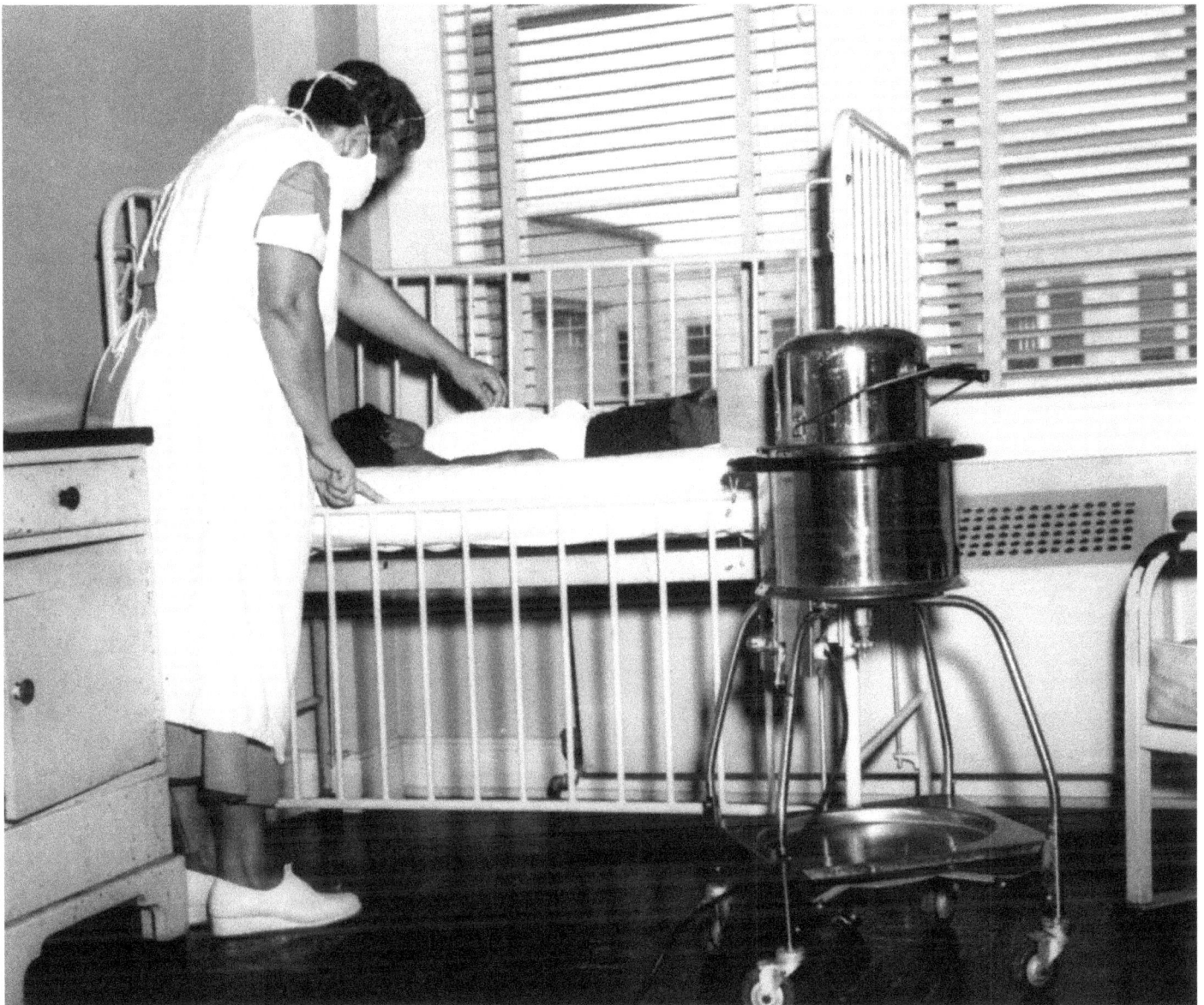

A nurse cares for a young patient in a hospital room. In the early 1950s Corpus Christi had nine hospitals including the U.S. Naval Hospital; Spohn Hospital, which opened in 1923; Memorial Hospital (1944); Driscoll Hospital; Thomas-Spann; Hilltop Tuberculosis Hospital (1953); Crippled Children's Hospital (1938); Corpus Christi Osteopathic Hospital; and the Osteopathic Hospital, which was a training facility.

Several men sit at the counter in this restaurant. Corpus Christi had several restaurants during this time to accommodate the growing population from the port development, the oil industry, and the Naval Air Station.

Four jets fly over the Administration Building at the Naval Air Station. This photograph portrays the well-established and manicured lawn in front of the building in 1957.

The opening of the Buccaneer Days begins with the reenactment of the discovery of Corpus Christi Bay.
These pirates and maids aboard this ship are making their way to the dock in 1957 for this ceremony.

Several residents take advantage of the shade outside the Cotton Jammers Corporation building in August of 1958.

The Harbor Bridge crosses the port of Corpus Christi in this aerial view taken on February 6, 1963.

A ship traveling through the port in April 1961 passes the Public Grain Elevators on the left. In 1954, an elevator with a two-million-bushel capacity was opened for storage in this area. In 1959, additional steel tanks were added, as seen in this picture, which increased storage capacity to 4,160,000 bushels. Additional grain elevators would be built several years later and further increase storage capacity by 1.5 million.

Men and women on horseback gear up for a parade. One of the wagons has a banner which reads "Sun, Sand & Surf—Corpus Christi Chamber of Commerce—Buccaneer Days."

Jim Wright, Howard Stulting, and Howard Stulting, Jr., on horseback, ready to leave on the South Texas Trail Ride. This trail ride began at the J & D Dude Ranch in Corpus Christi on its way to the 1964 Livestock Show and Rodeo in San Antonio.

The Commerce Building and Medical Professional Building at 416 North Chaparral towers over its neighbors. This nine-story structure built by W. E. Pope in 1929 had 175 offices, with the ninth floor used as a hospital. The tallest building in the area, it was sold in 1934 to Medical Professional Building Corporation and in 1965 to oil operators Ben D. Marks and O. D. Edwards and real estate entrepreneur Sheldon Katz.

This groundbreaking ceremony for the Ada Wilson Hospital of Physical Medicine and Rehabilitation was held on April 22, 1964, on the driveway of the Driscoll Foundation Children's Hospital. This facility located south of the Driscoll Hospital would be associated with the South Texas Children's Medical Center Foundation. The two speakers are Senator Bruce Reagan, who was master of ceremonies, and Dr. James L. Barnard, mayor.

A Corpus Christi patrolman provides an escort for these two buses traveling down Chaparral Street on October 24, 1964.

Chaparral Aviation, located in the Beechcraft Aviation Center at the Corpus Christi International Airport, provided a maintenance facility and stored aircraft.

This view of the Corpus Christi International Airport in 1964 features Gault Aviation. This aviation business was operated by Roger and Elaine Gault for 33 years. Both were pilots and served in the Civilian Pilot Training Program. This unique building style of a hyperbolic-paraboloid, designed by architect Joe L. Williams, housed their business for 15 years.

This offshore rig is drilling out in the bay for Forest Oil Company. The 1950s had witnessed a large amount of exploration, and several companies made their home in Corpus Christi. Forest Oil Company, founded by Clayton Dorn in 1926, moved to Corpus Christi by 1949 and operated for over 40 years in this area.

This 1964 view of busy Leopard Street highlights the Wilson Building. Originally the Nixon Building, built by Maston Nixon in 1926, it was purchased by Sam E. Wilson in 1947. The name changed to the Wilson Building, and five years later the Wilson tower was added. The sign for the Nixon Café is on the front of the building. It was a popular place for businesspeople to have lunch.

Ships travel across the port while an engineer and employees lower an instrument into the water.

The interior of the American Bottling Company at 717 Lester in 1965. This business was founded by S. W. Dunnam, Sr., who arrived in Corpus Christi in 1904. Originally opened on Water Street, it moved to 1001 Leopard in 1907, and a year later received the Coca-Cola franchise. The soda was bottled by hand until 1921, when semiautomatic equipment was installed. In 1939, the city's first vending machines stocked this popular soft drink.

Janet Grant stops to feed the Laughing Gulls near the bay. Laughing Gulls, quite prevalent in the area, entice tourists and residents to throw food in the air. Many people, especially children, like to hear their shrieks and watch them dive to catch a morsel of food sailing through the air.

A yacht sails across the bay just beyond the jetties. The skyline of the city is in the background.

The Jaycees of Corpus Christi sponsored Barbara Jones for a beauty contest along the bay.

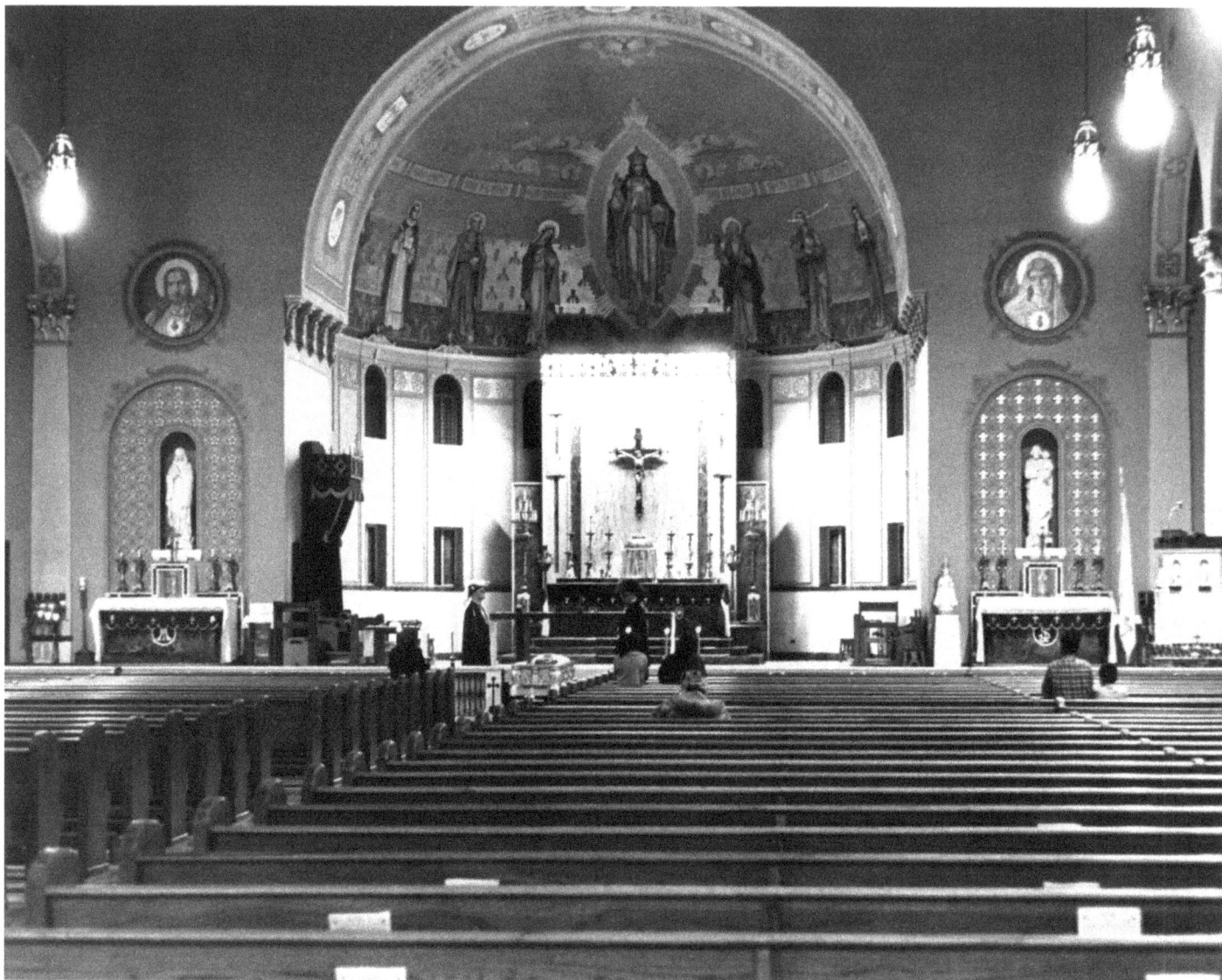

The body of Bishop Mariano S. Garriga lies in state in the Corpus Christi Cathedral. Born in 1886 at Port Isabel, he had been a priest for over 54 years and the first native Texan to be made bishop. He initiated a seminary in San Antonio and served as chaplain of the Texas Infantry in the Pershing expedition into Mexico and with the 144th Infantry in World War I. He was made Bishop in 1936 and served South Texas for many years.

Members of the Flour Bluff Fire Department aboard their truck.

This is the Charles W. Crossley Elementary School in 1965. The building, located at 2512 Koepke, was built in 1926 and has gone through several expansions and renovations. It was named for C. W. Crossley, who served for two years as a principal in Corpus Christi. In 1892, he was promoted to school superintendent and sought to improve the school system until his retirement in 1900.

Children seated around the Christmas tree, enjoying their snacks at the Carmelite Day Nursery. This nursery was opened in 1925 by four Carmelite Sisters. Since Corpus Christi did not have a nursery to care for children of working women, the sisters provided a necessary service. Their first building, a simple four-story frame house on Last Street (Buffalo and Alameda) expanded through the years to handle the growing population.

The Centennial House, built in the 1850s, was given to E. J. Davis and Ann Elizabeth Britton Davis as a wedding present from her father, Major Forbes Britton. E. J. Davis, a confirmed Unionist, lost his position as district judge during the Civil War because of his sentiments. After the war, he was part of two Texas Constitutional Conventions and in 1869 became the only candidate from Corpus Christi ever to win the gubernatorial election.

A crowd fills the inside of the Memorial Coliseum. This building designed by Richard Colley received its name in 1954 when the American Gold Star Mothers, a club for women who have lost children in war, placed a plaque on it to honor those lost in World War II. The building served as the city's social and political center for many years.

Two girls stand in front of the Nueces Hotel staring at a banner welcoming Dan Chamberlin.

This is a view of the Caller-Times Publishing Company, located at 820 Lower North Broadway. In 1928, Houston Harte and Bernard Hanks bought the 18-year-old *Corpus Christi Times* afternoon paper. A year later they purchased the *Corpus Christi Caller*, which had printed its first newspaper on January 21, 1883. The two papers merged and are now called the *Corpus Christi Caller-Times*, which operates out of this building.

Patrons line up in the post office, probably to mail Christmas packages. The boy is John David Parr. Mrs. Ethel Bryant and Mrs. Walton Tally are among those standing in line.

This is the United States Coast Guard Depot. The United States Government purchased a tract of land at the Port of Corpus Christi in the 1940s. This building allowed for more inspections of incoming vessels in the port area. The station was also used for repairing and painting buoys and other equipment.

The city council poses in front of the Memorial Coliseum in 1967.

NOTES ON THE PHOTOGRAPHS

These notes, listed by page number, attempt to include all aspects known of the photographs. Each of the photographs is identified by the page number, photograph's title or description, photographer and collection, archive, and call or box number when applicable. Although every attempt was made to collect all available data, in some cases complete data was unavailable due to the age and condition of some of the photographs and records.

II MARKET HALL
Special Collections & Archives, Texas A&M University-Corpus Christi, Bell Library, Meuly/ Daimwood Collection 108 Box 19

VI HARRISON COFFEE COMPANY
Corpus Christi Public Libraries Folder 9.10 Item 1

X PIPE BEING HAULED
Corpus Christi Public Libraries, Collection F1 Box 19 19.07 Item 13

2 THE HEADEN AND SONS BUILDING
Corpus Christi Public Libraries, Collection F1 Box 9 Folder 9.27 Item 1

3 DAVID HIRSCH HOUSE
Corpus Christi Public Libraries, Collection F1 Box 7 Folder 7.26 Item 1

4 LAGUNA STREET
Corpus Christi Public Libraries, Collection F1 Box 1 Folder 1.14 Item 1

5 HACK DRIVERS
Corpus Christi Public Libraries, Collection F1 Box 17 Folder 17.12 Item 1

6 ARTHUR H. EDEY & KIRSTEN
Corpus Christi Public Libraries, Collection F1 Box 9 Folder 9.26 Item 1

7 DERYEE DRUG STORE
Corpus Christi Public Libraries, Collection F1 Box 9 Folder 9.21 Item 3

8 CHAPARRAL STREET
Corpus Christi Public Libraries, Collection F1 Box 9 Folder 9.29 Item 1

9 DR. A. G. HEANEY HOUSE
Corpus Christi Public Libraries, Collection F1 Box 7 Folder 7.25 Item 1

10 HORSE AND CART
Corpus Christi Public Libraries, Collection B12 Box 1 Folder 1.01 Item 11

11 VOLUNTEER FIRE DEPARTMENT
Corpus Christi Public Libraries, Collection F5 Box 4 Folder 4.21 Item 10

12 C. C. MARKET HALL
Corpus Christi Public Libraries, Collection F1 Box 30 Folder 30.01 Item 1

13 FIRE DEPARTMENT AND SECURITY HOSE CO. NO. 3
Corpus Christi Public Libraries, Collection F5 Box 4 Folder 4.21 Item 2

14 SAINT PATRICK'S CATHOLIC CHURCH
Corpus Christi Public Libraries, Collection F1 Box 4 Folder 4.17 Item 2

15 ALTA VISTA HOTEL
Corpus Christi Public Libraries, Collection F1 Box 10 Folder 10.01 Item 6

16 CORPUS CHRISTI PUBLIC SCHOOL
Corpus Christi Public Libraries, Collection F1 Box 5 Folder 5.08 Item 1

18 WEATHER BUREAU
Corpus Christi Public Libraries, Collection F1 Box 6 Folder 6.26 Item 1

20 MARKET HALL
Corpus Christi Public Libraries, Collection F1 Box 6 Folder 6.05 Item 1

21 CORPUS CHRISTI NATIONAL BANK
Corpus Christi Public Libraries, Collection F1 Box 19 Folder 19.07 Item 1

22 MULE-DRAWN WATER CART
Special Collections & Archives, Texas A&M University-Corpus Christi, Bell Library, Kilgore Collection 7, 17.2.98 (c)

23 CORPUS CHRISTI PUBLIC SCHOOL GROUPS
Corpus Christi Public Libraries, Collection F5 Box 4 Folder 4.23 Item 4

24 CORPUS CHRISTI SHAMROCK HOSE COMPANY NO. 4
Corpus Christi Public Libraries, Collection F5 Folder 4.21 Item 13

25 HENRY KELLER SADDLER SHOP
Corpus Christi Public Libraries, Collection F1 Box 9 Folder 9.50 Item 1

26 HOLLUB COURTHOUSE
Special Collections & Archives, Texas A&M University-Corpus Christi, Bell Library, Kilgore Collection 7, 17.21 (c)

27 NUECES COUNTY JAIL
Special Collections & Archives, Texas A&M University-Corpus Christi, Bell Library, Kilgore Collection 7, 17.2.37 (a)

28 FIRST GRADE
Corpus Christi Public Libraries, Collection F5 Box 4 Folder 4.23 Items 1-3

29 BAYFRONT EARLY
Corpus Christi Public Libraries, Collection F1 Box 1 Folder 1.01 Item 13

30 FOOTBALL
Corpus Christi Public Libraries, Collection F1 Box 24 Folder 24.07 Item 1

31 EPWORTH INN
Corpus Christi Public Libraries, Collection F1 Box 10 Folder 10.04 Item 7

32 METHODIST CHURCH SUMMER CAMP
Special Collections & Archives, Texas A&M University-Corpus Christi, Bell Library, Meuly/Daimwood Collection 108 Box 19

34 DUNNE AMBULANCE
Corpus Christi Public Libraries, Collection F1 Box 17.05 Item 1

35 CULPEPPER HOUSE
Corpus Christi Public Libraries, Collection F1 Box 7 Folder 7.14 Item 1

36 WAGON
Special Collections & Archives, Texas A&M University-Corpus Christi, Bell Library, Kilgore Collection 7, 17.2.97

37 STATE HOTEL
Corpus Christi Public Libraries, Collection F1 Box 10 Folder 10.18 Item 4

38 EPWORTH INN
Corpus Christi Public Libraries, Collection F1 Box 10 Folder 10.04 Item 6

39 SPOHN SANITARIUM
Corpus Christi Public Libraries, Collection F1 Box 4 Folder 4.34 Item 1

40 CONVENT OF THE INCARNATE WORD ACADEMY
Corpus Christi Public Libraries, Collection F1 Box 4 Folder 4.17 Item 3

41 STEAM LAUNDRY AND DYE WORKS
Corpus Christi Public Libraries, Collection F1 Box 9 Folder 9.40 Item 2

42 GROUNDBREAKING
Special Collections & Archives, Texas A&M University-Corpus Christi, Bell Library, Meuly/Daimwood Collection 108 Box 24

43 W. H. DREYER MEAT MARKET
Corpus Christi Public Libraries, Collection F1 Box 9 Folder 9.07 Item 1

44 BAPTISM
Corpus Christi Public Libraries, Collection F1 Box Folder 4.07 Item 1

45 PITTS LIVERY COMPANY
Corpus Christi Public Libraries, Collection F1 Box 9 Folder 9.41 Item 1

46 HUNTERS
Special Collections & Archives, Texas A&M University-Corpus Christi, Bell Library, Meuly/Daimwood Collection 108 Box 24

47 BAYFRONT CENTRAL WHARF
Corpus Christi Public Libraries, Collection F1 Box 2 Folder 2.01 Item 7

48 "OLD NAT" WATERSLIDE
Corpus Christi Public Libraries, Collection F1 Box 2 Folder 2.10 Item 5

49 SIDBURY LUMBER COMPANY
Corpus Christi Public Libraries, Collection F1 Box9 Folder 9.42 Item 1

50 TEXAS WATERWAYS CONVENTION
Corpus Christi Public Libraries, Collection F5 Box 5 Folder 5.40 Item 1

51 BAYFRONT NORTH BEACH
Corpus Christi Public Libraries, Collection F1 Box 2 Folder 2.10 Item 6

52 CHAPARRAL EARLY IMAGES
Corpus Christi Public Libraries, Collection F1 Box 19 Folder 19.07 Item 7

53 STREETCARS/ TROLLEYS
Corpus Christi Public Libraries, Collection F1 Box 17 Folder 17.26 Item 2

54 BREAKERS HOTEL
Corpus Christi Public Libraries, Collection F1 Box 10 Folder 10.02 Item 1

55 WHITE POINT DRILLING WELLS BLOWOUT
Corpus Christi Public Libraries, Collection F1 Box 15 Folder 15.02 Item 1

56 CHAPARRAL STREET
Corpus Christi Public Libraries, Collection F1 Box 19 Folder 19.07 Item 4

57 CAHILL PLUMBING COMPANY
Corpus Christi Public Libraries, Collection F1Box 9 Folder 9.47 Item 1

58 HIGH SCHOOL FOOTBALL 1910
Corpus Christi Public Libraries, Collection F1 Box 24 Folder 24.07 Item 2

59 EARLY AIRPLANE
Corpus Christi Public Libraries, Collection F1 Box 17 Folder 17.01 Item 5

60 DOWNED PLANE
Corpus Christi Public Libraries, Collection F1 Box 3 Folder 3.02 Item 1

61 ALTA VISTA HOTEL
Corpus Christi Public Libraries, Collection F1 Box 10 Folder 10.01 Item 14

62 POLICE DEPARTMENT
Corpus Christi Public Libraries, Collection F1 Box 4 Folder 4.22 Item 1-3

63 BLUFF
Corpus Christi Public Libraries, Collection F1 Box 1 Folder 1.24 Item 2

64 TICKET OFFICE
Corpus Christi Public Libraries, Collection F1 Box 17 Folder 17.21 Item 1

65 DRAUGHONS CORPUS CHRISTI COLLEGE
Corpus Christi Public Libraries, Collection F1 Box 5 Folder 5.34 Item 1

66 STREETCAR
Corpus Christi Public Libraries, Collection F1 Box 17 Folder 17.26 Item 12

67 TRANSFER COMPANY
Corpus Christi Public Libraries, Collection F1 Box 9 Folder 9.24 Item 1

68 HORNE APARTMENTS
Corpus Christi Public Libraries, Collection F1 Box 10 Folder 10.05 Item 1

69 NUECES COUNTY COURTHOUSE
Corpus Christi Public Libraries, Collection F1 Box 6 Folder 6.14 Item 41

70 NUECES HOTEL
Corpus Christi Public Libraries, Collection F1 Box 10 Folder 10.11 Item 10

71 SEASIDE PAVILION HOTEL
Corpus Christi Public Libraries, Collection F1 Box 10 Folder 10.16 Item 8

72 1916 STORM
Corpus Christi Public Libraries, Collection F1 Box 29 Folder 29.01 Item 2

73 1916 STORM
Corpus Christi Public Libraries, Collection F1 Box 29 Folder 29.01 Item 4

74 SEA SCOUTS
Corpus Christi Public Libraries, Collection F1 Box 4 Folder 4.09 Item 3

75 TROLLEY
Corpus Christi Public Libraries, Collection F1 Box 17 Folder 17.26 Item 9

76 HOUSE
Corpus Christi Public Libraries, Collection F1 Box 7 Folder 7.39 Item 6

77 1919 STORM
Corpus Christi Public Libraries, Collection F1 Box 29 Folder 29.05 Item 9

78 1919 HURRICANE
Special Collections & Archives, Texas A&M University-Corpus Christi, Bell Library, Kilgore Collection 7, 17.2.79 (b)

80 CLEANUP
Special Collections & Archives, Texas A&M University-Corpus Christi, Bell Library, Kilgore Collection 7, 17.2.79 (b)

81 1919 HURRICANE
Special Collections & Archives, Texas A&M University-Corpus Christi, Bell Library, Kilgore Collection 7, 17.2.79 (b)

82 BAYFRONT NORTH BEACH
Corpus Christi Public Libraries, Collection F1 Box 2 Folder 2.11 Item 4

83 CHURCH OF THE GOOD SHEPHERD
Corpus Christi Public Libraries ,Collection F1 Box 4 Folder 4.04 Item 1

84 BIDWELL HOTEL
Corpus Christi Public Libraries, Collection F1 Box 20 Folder 20.01 Item 1

85 INCARNATE WORD ACADEMY
Corpus Christi Public Libraries, Collection F1 Box 5 Folder 5.06 Item 3

86 STATE NATIONAL BANK
Corpus Christi Public Libraries, Collection F1 Box 6 Folder 6.32 Item 1

87 SIMON-COHN COMPANY
Corpus Christi Public Libraries, Collection F1 Box 9 Folder 9.18 Item 1

88 MEEHANS DRY GOODS COMPANY
Corpus Christi Public Libraries, Collection F1 Box 9 Folder 9.15 Item 1

90 OPENING CEREMONY
Corpus Christi Public Libraries, Collection F1 Box 12 Folder 12.02 Item 1

91 OPENING CEREMONY
Corpus Christi Public Libraries, Collection F1 Box 12 Folder 12.02 Item 3

92 W. W. JONES HOUSE
Corpus Christi Public Libraries, Collection F1 Box 7 Folder 7.27 Item 1

93 SMITH ELECTRIC COMPANY
Corpus Christi Public Libraries, Collection F1 Box 9 Folder 9.22 Item 1

94 SOUTH TEXAS CANDY CO.
Corpus Christi Public Libraries, Collection F1 Box 9 Folder 9.08 Item 1

95 NUECES COFFEE COMPANY
Corpus Christi Public Libraries, Collection F1 Box 9 Folder 9.11 Item 2

96 BUSINESSES
Corpus Christi Public Libraries, Collection F1 Box 9 Folder 9.58 Item 7

97 ACME CONCRETE PIPE CO.
Corpus Christi Public Libraries, Collection F1 Box 13 Folder 13.01 Item 1

98 BLUFF
Corpus Christi Public Libraries ,Collection F1 Box 1 Folder 1.24 Item 4

99 PIER CAFE
Corpus Christi Public Libraries, Collection F1 Box 11 Folder 11.06 Item 1

100 BORDEN COMPANY
Corpus Christi Public Libraries, Collection F1 Box 9 Folder 9.43 Item 1

101 SOUTHERN PACIFIC
RAIL LINE
Corpus Christi Public
Libraries, Collection F1 Box
17 Folder 17.20 Item 1

102 NUECES HARDWARE
COMPANY
Corpus Christi Public
Libraries, Collection F1 Box
9 Folder 9.33 Item 1

103 BAYFRONT
BREAKWATER/JETTIES
Corpus Christi Public
Libraries, Collection F1 Box
2 Folder 1 Item 1

104 NUECES HOTEL
Corpus Christi Public
Libraries, Collection F1 Box
10 Folder 10.11 Item 12

105 BAYFRONT NORTH BEACH
Corpus Christi Public
Libraries, Collection F1 Box
2 Folder 2.12 Item 1

106 RESTAURANT
Corpus Christi Public
Libraries
Photo by Doc McGregor
Collection F1 Box 11 Folder
11.11 Item 3

107 NUECES HOTEL
Corpus Christi Public
Libraries, Collection F1 Box
10 Folder 10.11 Item 8

108 CORPUS CHRISTI
ACADEMY
Corpus Christi Public
Libraries, Collection F1 Box
5 Folder 5.05 Item 1

109 BROADWAY
Corpus Christi Public
Libraries, Collection F1 Box
19 Folder 19.03 Item 1

110 KIWANIS CLUB
Corpus Christi Public
Libraries, Collection F1 Box
5 Folder 5.04 Item 1

111 CITY NATIONAL BANK
Corpus Christi Public
Libraries, Collection F1 Box
6 Folder 6.29 Item 1

112 BAYFRONT PLEASURE
PIER
Corpus Christi Public
Libraries, Collection F1 Box
2 Folder 2.03 Item 2

113 ST. PATRICK'S
CATHEDRAL
Corpus Christi Public
Libraries, Collection F1 Box
5 Folder 5.36 Item 1

114 FISHING
Library of Congress
LC-USF34-034510-D

115 SHOE STORE
Corpus Christi Public
Libraries
Photo by Doc McGregor
Collection F1 Box 9 Folder
9.58 Item 5

116 LICHTENSTEIN'S
DEPARTMENT STORE
Corpus Christi Public
Libraries, Collection F1 Box
9 Folder 9.13 Item 1

118 NAVAL AIR STATION
Corpus Christi Public
Libraries, Collection F1 Box
6 Folder 6.24 Item 1

119 ROTC IN PARADE
Corpus Christi Public
Libraries, Collection F1 Box
25 Folder 25.01 Item 1

120 DRIVE-IN
Library of Congress
LC-USF34-038273-D

121 RESIDENCE
Corpus Christi Public
Libraries, Collection F1 Box
8 Folder 8.06 Item 12

122 NAP
Corpus Christi Public
Libraries, Collection F1 Box
2 Folder 2.13 Item 14

123 DRAUGHONS PRACTICAL
BUSINESS COLLEGE
Corpus Christi Public
Libraries, Collection F1 Box
5 Folder 5.34 Item 2

124 HIGH SCHOOL
BUCCANEER FOOTBALL
Corpus Christi Public
Libraries, Collection F1 Box
24 Folder 24.07 Item 7

125 CORPUS CHRISTI NAVAL
HOSPITAL
Corpus Christi Public
Libraries, Collection F1 Box
4 Folder 4.25 Item 1

126 SOUTHERN PAINT
SUPPLY
Corpus Christi Public
Libraries, Collection F1 Box
9 Folder 9.45 Item 1

127 U.S. POST OFFICE
Corpus Christi Public
Libraries, Collection F1 Box
6 Folder 6.25 Item 1

128 LIGHTHOUSE CAFE
Corpus Christi Public
Libraries, Collection F1 Box
11 Folder 11.04 Item 2

129 NAVY AD
Special Collections &
Archives, Texas A&M
University-Corpus Christi,
Bell Library, Smiley
Collection 9, 2.12

130 DRUG STORE
Special Collections &
Archives, Texas A&M
University-Corpus Christi,
Bell Library, Smiley
Collection 9, 26.6

132 AMUSEMENT PARK
Special Collections &
Archives, Texas A&M
University-Corpus Christi,
Bell Library, Smiley
Collection 9, 29.6

133 PILOT
Special Collections &
Archives, Texas A&M
University-Corpus Christi,
Bell Library, Smiley
Collection 9, 26.6

134 U.S. NAVY
Special Collections &
Archives, Texas A&M
University-Corpus Christi,
Bell Library, Smiley
Collection 9, 29.20

135 WAVES
Special Collections &
Archives, Texas A&M
University-Corpus Christi,
Bell Library, Smiley
Collection 9, 29.3 (McGregor
Studio)

136 BUILDING A PLANE
Special Collections &
Archives, Texas A&M
University-Corpus
Christi, Bell Library,
Smiley Collection 9, 29.23
(McGregor Studio)

138 **AERIAL VIEW**
Corpus Christi Public
Libraries, Collection F1 Box
1 Folder 1.26 Item 2

139 **RELAXING**
Special Collections &
Archives, Texas A&M
University-Corpus Christi,
Bell Library, Smiley
Collection 9, 26.6 (McGregor
Studio)

140 **EL PATIO MEXICAN
FOOD**
Corpus Christi Public
Libraries, Collection F1 Box
11 Folder 11.02 Item 1

141 **RED CROSS**
Special Collections &
Archives, Texas A&M
University-Corpus Christi,
Bell Library, Smiley
Collection 9, 26.6 (McGregor
Studio)

142 **RADIO TELEPHONE**
Library of Congress
LC-USW3-034012

143 **NAVAL AIR BASE**
Special Collections &
Archives, Texas A&M
University-Corpus Christi,
Bell Library, Smiley
Collection 9, 26.6 (McGregor
Studio)

144 **NAVY BAND**
Special Collections &
Archives, Texas A&M
University-Corpus Christi,
Bell Library, Smiley
Collection 9, 26.6 (McGregor
Studio)

145 **CORPUS CHRISTI FIRE
DEPARTMENT**
Corpus Christi Public
Libraries, Collection F1 Box
4 Folder 4.21 Item 11

146 **UPPER BROADWAY**
Corpus Christi Public
Libraries, Collection F1 Box
1 Folder 1.26 Item 10

147 **ADMIRAL C. W. NIMITZ**
Corpus Christi Public
Libraries, Collection F1 Box
27 Folder 27.10 Item 1

148 **DR. E. L. HARVIN**
Corpus Christi Public
Libraries, Collection F1 Box
5 Folder 5.32 Item 7

149 **CHURCH OF GOOD
SHEPHERD**
Corpus Christi Public
Libraries, Collection F1 Box
4 Folder 4.04 Item 5

150 **CAMP FIRE GIRLS**
Special Collections &
Archives, Texas A&M
University-Corpus Christi,
Bell Library, Smiley
Collection 9, 26.6 (McGregor
Studio)

152 **BLUE ANGELS**
Corpus Christi Public
Libraries, Collection F1 Box
1 Folder 1.11 Item 6

153 **HECTOR P. GARCIA**
Special Collections &
Archives, Texas A&M
University-Corpus Christi,
Bell Library
Garcia Collection 5

154 **NORTH GATE SENTRY
HOUSE**
Corpus Christi Public
Libraries, Collection F1 Box
27 Folder 27.11 Item 1

156 **BROADWAY**
Corpus Christi Public
Libraries, Collection F1 Box
1 Folder 1.27 Item 1

157 **C. C. JUNIOR COLLEGE**
Corpus Christi Public
Libraries, Collection F1 Box
5 Folder 5.32 Item 17

158 **LA RETAMA PUBLIC
LIBRARY BOOKMOBILE**
Corpus Christi Public
Libraries, Collection F1 Box
4 Folder 4.40 Item 13

159 **W. W. JONES HOUSE**
Corpus Christi Public
Libraries, Collection F1 Box
4 Folder 4.40 Item 4

160 **JOE J. ALSUP**
Corpus Christi Public
Libraries, Collection F1 Box
6 Folder 6.47 Item 6

161 **CORPUS CHRISTI TRUST
COMPANY**
Corpus Christi Public
Libraries, Collection F1 Box
6 Folder 6.30 Item 2

162 **CORPUS CHRISTI BANK
AND TRUST COMPANY**
Corpus Christi Public
Libraries, Collection F1 Box
6 Folder 6.30 Item 5

163 **FIRST BAPTIST CHURCH**
Corpus Christi Public
Libraries, Collection F1 Box
4 Folder 4.07 Item 3

164 **PORT OF CORPUS
CHRISTI**
Corpus Christi Public
Libraries, Collection F1 Box
12 Folder 12.14 Item 19

165 **DEL MAR COLLEGE**
Corpus Christi Public
Libraries, Collection F1 Box
5 Folder 5.32 Item 21

166 **CONSTRUCTION**
Corpus Christi Public
Libraries, Collection F1 Box
21 Folder 21.04 Item 1

167 **NUECES HOTEL**
Corpus Christi Public
Libraries, Collection F1 Box
Folder 10.11 Item 5

168 **LOU TURBEVILLE**
Corpus Christi Public
Libraries, Collection F1 Box
24 Folder 24.03 Item 1

169 **HOSPITAL**
Corpus Christi Public
Libraries, Collection F1 Box
4 Folder 4.35 Item 1

170 **RESTAURANT**
Corpus Christi Public
Libraries, Collection F1 Box
11 Folder 11.11 Item 1

171 **MILITARY HISTORY**
Corpus Christi Public
Libraries, Collection F1 Box
27 Folder 27.11 Item 2

172 **PIRATES AND PIRATE
MAIDS**
Corpus Christi Public
Libraries, Collection F1 Box
25 Folder 25.02 Item 1

173 COTTON JAMMERS
     CORPORATION
Corpus Christi Public
Libraries, Collection F1 Box
9 Folder 9.57 Item 1

174 HARBOR BRIDGE
Corpus Christi Public
Libraries, Collection F1 Box
9 Folder 9.57 Item 1

175 AERIAL
Corpus Christi Public
Libraries, Collection F1 Box
12 Folder 12.11 Item 1

176 INDIVIDUALS ON
     HORSEBACK
Corpus Christi Public
Libraries, Collection F1 Box
24 Folder 24.15 Item 2

177 HORSEBACK
Corpus Christi Public
Libraries, Collection F1 Box
24 Folder 24.15 Item 5

178 COMMERCE BUILDING
Corpus Christi Public
Libraries, Collection F1 Box
6 Folder 6.37 Item 2

179 ADA WILSON HOSPITAL
Corpus Christi Public
Libraries, Collection F1 Box
4 Folder 4.22 Item 3

180 PATROLMAN
Corpus Christi Public
Libraries, Collection F1 Box
4 Folder 4.22 Item 6

181 CUDDIHY FIELD
Corpus Christi Public
Libraries, Collection F1 Box
17 Folder 17.04 Item 1

182 INTERNATIONAL
     AIRPORT
Corpus Christi Public
Libraries, Collection F1 Box
17 Folder 17.03 Item 6

183 OFFSHORE DRILLING
Corpus Christi Public
Libraries, Collection F1 Box
15 Folder 15.05 Item 1

184 WILSON TOWER
     BUILDING
Corpus Christi Public
Libraries, Collection F1 Box
6 Folder 6.47 Item 2

185 WORKERS
Corpus Christi Public
Libraries, Collection F1 Box
14 Folder 14.20 Item 46

186 AMERICAN BOTTLING
     COMPANY
Corpus Christi Public
Libraries, Collection F1 Box
9 Folder 9.04 Item 1

187 BAYFRONT MARINA
Corpus Christi Public
Libraries, Collection F1 Box
2 Folder 2.05 Item 2

188 BAYFRONT MARINA
Corpus Christi Public
Libraries, Collection F1 Box
2 Folder 2.05 Item 17

189 JAYCEES OF CORPUS
     CHRIST
Corpus Christi Public
Libraries, Collection F1 Box
4 Folder 4.05 Item 5

190 BISHOP GARRIGA LYING
     IN STATE
Corpus Christi Public
Libraries, Collection F1 Box
2 Folder 2.17 Item 1

191 FLOUR BLUFF FIRE
     DEPARTMENT
Corpus Christi Public
Libraries, Collection F1 Box
4 Folder 4.21 Item 12

192 C. W. CROSSLEY
     ELEMENTARY
Corpus Christi Public
Libraries, Collection F1 Box
5 Folder 5.10 Item 2

193 CARMELITE SISTERS
     DAY NURSERY
Corpus Christi Public
Libraries, Collection F1 Box
5 Folder 5.04 Item 3

194 THE CENTENNIAL
     HOUSE
Corpus Christi Public
Libraries, Collection F1 Box
7 Folder 7.07 Item 7

195 MEMORIAL COLISEUM
Corpus Christi Public
Libraries, Collection F1 Box
6 Folder 6.10 Item 19

196 NUECES HOTEL
Corpus Christi Public
Libraries, Collection F1 Box
10 Folder 10.11 Item 13

197 THE CALLER-TIMES
     PUBLISHING COMPANY
Corpus Christi Public
Libraries, Collection F1 Box
9 Folder 9.49 Item 1

198 POST OFFICE
Corpus Christi Public
Libraries, Collection F1 Box
5 Folder 5.43 Item 3

199 UNITED STATES COAST
     GUARD
Corpus Christi Public
Libraries, Collection F1 Box
6 Folder 6.23 Item 1

200 MEMORIAL COLISEUM
Corpus Christi Public
Libraries, Collection F1 Box
4 Folder 4.15 Item 26

HISTORIC PHOTOS OF
CORPUS CHRISTI

Bay breezes from the Gulf of Mexico sweep into this sparkling city by the sea. The sound of the wind, waves, and shore birds transport harmonic music to the ears of those who walk its beaches and parks. Corpus Christi, Texas, one of the most pristine coastal cities, lies at the mouth of the Nueces River, and from its humble beginnings as a simple nineteenth-century trading post, it has developed into a major city. Farming and ranching, the railroad, port, Naval Air Station, and the oil and gas industry have aided this city in realizing its growth potential.

Historic Photos of Corpus Christi brings to life the evolution of this growing community through nearly two hundred black-and-white photographs, drawn from a wide pool of topics to depict the history of the people, community, events, and businesses that have shaped this area. The rarely seen images gleaned from several archives provide a unique opportunity to peer into the past and discover the richness of this South Texas city.

Cecilia Gutierrez Venable has loved Corpus Christi for over thirty years. She earned a bachelor's degree in history from Texas A&M Corpus Christi University. As a graduate assistant at Texas A&M University Special Collections and Archives, she processed several collections and was instrumental in acquiring collections for the university. A research project later led her to the Corpus Christi Public Libraries Local History Room, where she found a wealth of information in their Special Collections. Under a grant-funded project, as well as numerous volunteer hours, she helped organize their manuscript collection, and acquired additional collections for this institution. She has worked as an archivist for the past eight years and has also served on the Nueces County Historical Society board, as well as the Nueces County Historical Commission. Venable is currently writing her thesis for a master's of philosophy in history.

WWW.TURNERPUBLISHING.COM

9781684420049